D1191041

Date Due

~~OCT 2 1 2003~~			
NOV 1 1 2003			

REGENTS RENAISSANCE DRAMA SERIES

General Editor: Cyrus Hoy
Advisory Editor: G. E. Bentley

THE LONGER THOU LIVEST
and
ENOUGH IS AS GOOD AS A FEAST

W. WAGER

The Longer Thou Livest
and
Enough Is as Good as a Feast

Edited by

R. Mark Benbow

UNIVERSITY OF NEBRASKA PRESS · LINCOLN

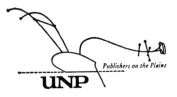

MANUFACTURED IN THE UNITED STATES OF AMERICA

Regents Renaissance Drama Series

The purpose of the Regents Renaissance Drama Series is to provide soundly edited texts, in modern spelling, of the more significant plays of the Elizabethan, Jacobean, and Caroline theater. Each text in the series is based on a fresh collation of all sixteenth- and seventeenth-century editions. The textual notes, which appear above the line at the bottom of each page, record all substantive departures from the edition used as the copy-text. Variant substantive readings among sixteenth- and seventeenth-century editions are listed there as well. In cases where two or more of the old editions present widely divergent readings, a list of substantive variants in editions through the seventeenth century is given in an appendix. Editions after 1700 are referred to in the textual notes only when an emendation originating in some one of them is received into the text. Variants of accidentals (spelling, punctuation, capitalization) are not recorded in the notes. Contracted forms of characters' names are silently expanded in speech prefixes and stage directions, and, in the case of speech prefixes,are regularized. Additions to the stage directions of the copy-text are enclosed in brackets. Stage directions such as "within" or "aside" are enclosed in parentheses when they occur in the copy-text.

Spelling has been modernized along consciously conservative lines. "Murther" has become "murder," and "burthen," "burden," but within the limits of a modernized text, and with the following exceptions, the linguistic quality of the original has been carefully preserved. The variety of contracted forms ('em, 'am, 'm, 'um, 'hem) used in the drama of the period for the pronoun *them* are here regularly given as 'em, and the alternation between a'th' and o'th' (for on or of the) is regularly reproduced as o'th'. The copy-text distinction between preterite endings in -d and -ed is preserved except where the elision of e occurs in the penultimate syllable; in such cases, the final syllable is contracted. Thus, where the old editions read "threat'ned," those of the present series read "threaten'd." Where, in the old editions, a contracted preterite in -y'd would yield -i'd in modern spelling (as in "try'd," "cry'd," "deny'd"), the word is here given in its full form (e.g., "tried," "cried," "denied").

Punctuation has been brought into accord with modern practices. The effort here has been to achieve a balance between the generally light pointing of the old editions, and a system of punctuation which, without overloading the text with exclamation marks, semicolons, and dashes, will make the often loosely flowing verse (and prose) of the original syntactically intelligible to the modern reader. Dashes are regularly used only to indicate interrupted speeches, or shifts of address within a single speech.

Explanatory notes, chiefly concerned with glossing obsolete words and phrases, are printed below the textual notes at the bottom of each page. References to stage directions in the notes follow the admirable system of the Revels editions, whereby stage directions are keyed, decimally, to the line of the text before or after which they occur. Thus, a note on 0.2 has reference to the second line of the stage direction at the beginning of the scene in question. A note on 115.1 has reference to the first line of the stage direction following line 115 of the text of the relevant scene.

CYRUS HOY

University of Rochester

Contents

List of Abbreviations

Bible, 1551   *The byble, that is to saye, all the holye scripture* ["Matthew Version"], 1551.

Brandl   A. Brandl, ed. "The Longer Thou Livest The More Fool Thou Art," *Shakespeare Jahrbuch*, XXXVI (1900).

Cooper   Thomas Cooper. *Thesaurus Linguae Romanae et Britannicae*. 1565.

Craik   T. Craik. *The Tudor Interlude*. Leicester, 1962.

Dickens   A. G. Dickens. *The English Reformation*. New York, 1964.

OED   *Oxford English Dictionary*

Q   quarto

S.D.   stage direction

S.P.   speech prefix

Stow   J. Stow. *Survey of London*, ed. C. L. Kingsford. Oxford, 1908.

Tilley   M. P. Tilley. *A Dictionary of the Proverbs in England in the Sixteenth and Seventeenth Centuries*. Ann Arbor, 1950.

Introduction

The first notice of W. Wager's *The Longer Thou Livest* is the entry in the Register of the Stationers' Company around April, 1569:

Jonnes   Recevyd of *Rychard Jonnes* for his lycense for pryntinge
of a ballett *the lenger thou leveste the more ffoole thow*   iiij$^{d\,1}$

Presumably soon after, the play was printed with the following title page:

[Within lace border] A very mery and/ Pythie Commedie, called *The longer/ thou liuest, the more foole thou art./* A Myrour very necessarie for youth, and/ specially for such as are like to come to dig-/ nitie and promotion: As it maye/ well appeare in the Matter/ folowynge./ Newly compiled by/ VV. VVager./ [ornament] *IMPRINTED AT/ London, by Wyllyam HoW/* for Richarde Johnes: and/ are to be solde at his shop/ under the Lotterie/ house.

Perhaps the following year, a second play, *Enough Is as Good as a Feast*, appeared without entry in the Register.[2] The title page reads in part:

A Comedy or Enter/ *lude intituled, Inough is as good as a feast,/* very fruteful godly and ful of plea-/ sant mirth. Compiled by/ W. Wager./ ... *IMPRINTED AT LON/* don at the long shop adioyning vnto S./ *Mildreds Church in the Pultrie,/* by John Allde.

In both cases the author's name is given as W. Wager, but beyond

1 E. Arber, ed., *A Transcript of the Registers of the Company of Stationers of London: 1554–1640 A.D.* (London, 1875–1894), I, 386.

2 William Jackson in the forthcoming revision of the *Short Title Catalogue* dates the play [1570?]; the play may have been recorded in the Register but the entry lost, since there is a lacuna in the records from July 22, 1571, to July 17, 1576 (W. W. Greg, *Bibliography of the English Printed Drama* [London, 1939], I, 5).

the ascription of these two plays to him, nothing further is known of the playwright.[3]

Although E. N. S. Thompson suggests that *The Longer* is "a revision of some old, full-scope moral play,"[4] the sources of both *The Longer* and *Enough* lie in contemporary materials which have been grafted upon the dramatic formulas of the moral interlude. The relation of *Enough* to the anonymous *Trial of Treasure* (1567) illustrates that it is less a question of borrowing than of adaptation. The two plays have some seventy-four lines in common which occur in scenes parallel in content but different in technique.[5] In *Trial* the characters Just, Trust, and Contentation appear in a static tableau midway through the play. In speeches which are largely direct address, they define the theological assumptions of the play. Wager moves their sermon to the beginning of his play and translates it into dramatic action. The theological discussion of Heavenly Man and Contentation becomes an argument which precipitates the conversion of Worldly Man and thus initiates the action of the play. In the process of adaptation, Wager recasts the dialogue of the *Trial* and increases the tension through the cut and thrust of the argument.

The most obvious of the non-dramatic sources is some edition of the "Matthew" Bible, a version prepared by John Rogers and first published in 1537. While neither play dramatizes a specific Biblical incident, the language and themes of both echo Scripture. In addition both plays draw upon homiletic materials. The general point of view in *Enough* is parallel to that in the *Exposition upon the Fifth, Sixth, and Seventh Chapters of Matthew* (1532), written by William Tyndale, the

[3] Although the *Dictionary of National Biography* calls him William, there is no evidence that this was his baptismal name. Two other plays have been attributed to Wager: *The Cruel Debtor* (*c.* 1566) and *The Trial of Treasure* (1567). The evidence for Wager's authorship of the former is inconclusive (W. W. Greg, *Collections* [Malone Society] I, iv–v, 316); and Leslie Oliver's argument for the authorship of *The Trial* depends upon similarities which are insignificant or traditional characteristics of the moral interlude ("William Wager and The Trial of Treasure," *Huntington Library Quarterly*, IX [1946], 419 ff.).

[4] E. N. S. Thompson, *The English Moral Plays* (New Haven, 1910), p. 398.

[5] *Enough*, ll. 121–280; *Trial*, Ciiij–Dii. Wager adds eighty-one lines and omits forty-seven. Of the seventy-four lines in common, only twenty-two are the same; forty-six have variants while six are variant lines. Cf. Oliver, pp. 419 ff.; the borrowing was first noted by L. B. Wright, "Social Aspects of Some Belated Morality Plays," *Anglia*, LIV (1930), 116.

Biblical translator and Reformer. For both play and homily the problem of wealth lies less in wealth itself than in the attitude toward wealth; indeed, as Tyndale points out, "riches is the gift of God, given to man to maintain the degrees of the world, and therefore not evil; yes, and some must be poor and some rich, if we shall have an order in this world."[6] What occasions the attack from the pulpit and in the traditional satiric "complaint" is the contemporary misuse of wealth. The sermons of Hugh Latimer, especially the Sermon on the Plough (January 18, 1548) and the two sermons before King Edward and his Council in Lent, 1550, are perhaps echoed throughout *Enough*, and the characters of the Tenant and the Hireling are common in secular satire. If the immediate sources of *The Longer* are less obvious, its thesis had often been propounded. In his ecclesiastical injunctions of 1536, Thomas Cromwell urged parents to educate children and to apprentice them to some honest occupation; failure to do so, Cromwell argued, would breed crime and social disorder. Moros himself belongs to the satiric tradition of *The Ship of Fools* and *The Praise of Folly*. Whatever the particular sources may be, Wager uses them to refurbish the dramatic formulas which were readily available.

By defining the symbolic mode within which the plays of the sixteenth century operate, recent research has done much to alter the view that these plays are crude, tedious lectures, intermittently redeemed by non-instructive entertainment.[7] The difficulty for the modern reader is to visualize the totality of production and to remember that the proscenium arch and its implicit search for realistic drama is still in the future. The strolling players for whom Wager designed his plays demanded little for a stage—a bare platea before the hall screen in a private home or inn, or a trestle stage with simple curtains or mansions; but their plays could be mounted for more splendid court performances. What is common to all settings is the symbolic mode in which the stage, if representing the earth, still suggests the eternal dimensions of the medieval universe. Within

[6] *Expositions and Notes on Sundry Portions of the Holy Scriptures* . . . , ed. H. Walter, Parker Society, XLIII (1849), p. 18.

[7] The important books upon which the following paragraphs are based are: D. Bevington, *From Mankind to Marlowe* (Cambridge, Mass., 1962); T. Craik, *The Tudor Interlude* (Leicester, 1962); B. Spivak, *Shakespeare and the Allegory of Evil* (New York, 1958); and G. Wickham, *Early English Stages* (*London*, 1959, 1962).

the symbolic mode, as Craik points out, costume is as much a metaphor as stage furniture, for costumes, even when decorative, are symbols whose meaning is unequivocal. Prophets, philosophers, virtues, and type characters wear their distinctive garbs and mingle with vicious abstractions in the robes of popery, and devils in masks or vizors. Traditionally the actor doubles, and he is recognized on stage not as a particular actor but as a character whose identity is established by his clothing or by the symbolic properties he carries. The small wardrobes of traveling companies tended to reinforce the symbolic mode since the costumes for one moral interlude could be used in another. Moreover, costume becomes a part of the action of the play and helps to define the symbolic or allegoric progression of the action. A change in costume serves to punctuate plot developments.

While his medieval predecessors had "unlimited" funds and personnel for spectacular shows, the sixteenth-century playwright who sought to provide plays for a symbolic theater was faced by serious limitations. He had to achieve maximum scope with minimum means. Since the size of a company, "four men and a boy," meant that actors must double if an action of scope was to be presented, the structure of plays had to accommodate doubling. Dramatic formulas emerged by which the medieval morality was adapted to the new conditions.[8] The central action remained the spiritual pilgrimage of man which involved some sort of medieval Psychomachia, the conflict between vices and virtues for the soul of man. The size of the company, however, forced the playwright to develop formulas for the alternation and suppression of characters. Because those who played the vices must also play the virtues, the forces of good and evil could not easily be brought into confrontation, and there was a tendency to alternate elevated discourse with comic merriment. To explore and expand the significance of the allegory, characters must be suppressed to make way for new characters played by the same actors. Since there could be no scene of assembly at the end of the play where all characters meet and where the complications of the plot could be unravelled, plot was designed to develop in a linear progression of episodes which culminated in a final exposition of the allegory. To bridge scenes, the playwright used soliloquy or direct address which preserved continuity while providing opportunity for change of costume. Drawing upon the tradition of pulpit oratory,

8 Bevington, Chap. 8.

such a device reinforced the expository nature of the play. Although the limited size of the company encouraged the development of a central vice, the use of alternate names for the vice and his subordinates created the illusion of a larger number of characters and more importantly extended the significance of the action. Whatever the formulas might be, they were governed by the symbolic mode. In the hands of the Tudor playwrights the medieval inheritance was given new relevance to daily life—theological metaphysics seemed to give way to social satire, the eschatological vision seemed to narrow, there was less concern with the holy dying and more with holy living—but the drama continued to develop the symbolic mode.

Both of Wager's plays are vehicles for dramatic commentary on social and political conditions. In one sense the gospel story has given way to controversial debate, theology to social and political morality. But such divisions are modern; for the sixteenth century religion and politics were not separate compartments. The popular preachers, Latimer and Bradford, conceive of the commonwealth within a religious context, and the discussion of the social problems of idleness and of the use of capital are couched in the theological concept of "vocation." If in *Enough* prodigality becomes a bogie, greed evil, and ambition a greater pride,[9] such issues are only the material out of which Wager constructs the story of the damnation of Worldly Man. Likewise, *The Longer* is a tract on education which attacks idleness and the lack of discipline at home and in school. Its immediate relevance is defined in part by the Statute of Artificers passed in 1563 which attempted to regulate the economy and to alleviate the problem of vagabonds. But *The Longer* is more than a tract, for it explores through the dramatic formulas the life of Moros the fool. If the plays are satiric, their basic metaphor remains that of the spiritual pilgrimage, and it is this metaphor which determines the structure of the plays.[10]

The Longer divides into three unequal sections depicting the fool as youth (ll. 71–1005), adult (ll. 1201–1684), and old man (ll. 1743–1890). Although half the play is devoted to Moros as youth, this should not mislead us into assuming that the play is a "youth play," concerned primarily with education, for in both plays Wager allots the opening section disproportionate space in order to define the

[9] Wright, p. 111.

[10] The following discussion draws upon the analyses of Bevington, pp. 158–65, and Craik, pp. 100–10.

issues. In the opening section the alternation of virtues and vices is emphasized by the parallelism of comic devices. In each part there is repetition which is wittily nonsensical or blasphemous, punning on names which serves to extend the symbolic significance, and each side provides "an order of instruction" for the education of Moros, symbolized by the Testament and by the pack of cards. The danger of mechanical alternation, however, is avoided by variation. In the bridge between sections one and two the dialogue of Fortune and Incontinence is framed by the addresses of Discipline and Piety. Moreover, in the second section, since Moros is committed to folly, the pattern of alternation is suppressed, and the section reverses the organization of the first so that the viciousness of Moros' folly is emphasized. In spite of his limited cast, Wager achieves partial confrontation of the opposing forces in sections one and two, and thus heightens the sense of conflict.

The possibility for confrontation is limited because, although Idleness seems to assume the role of a central vice in the opening section, there is indeed no central vice in the play who can distract our attention from the hero. Idleness, Incontinence, and Wrath give way to Ignorance, Impiety, and Cruelty; and the suppression reinforces the symbolic progression which defines the folly of the hero. The dominance of the hero, established in the opening sequence where Moros appears first with the three virtues and then with the three vices, is strengthened as Moros is isolated from both vices and virtues until in the final sequence he stands alone confronting the devils. The costume changes serve to point up the progression. While Moros' beard is an index of his chronological age, his clothing signifies his moral decline. The clothing of the extravagant gallant with the ostentatious red feather is replaced by the fool's suit in the final section. The play closes to be sure with the learned discussion of the virtues, but it is the damnation of Moros which holds our attention.

If the basic metaphor of the play is the traditional spiritual pilgrimage, there is no salvation for the fool and the play is tragic. It is not that Wager is more secular than his predecessors, but rather that he is using the traditional metaphors within a different set of assumptions. Insisting upon a personal approach to the religious experience and consequently asserting the priesthood of all believers, the Reformation rejected the institutionalism of the medieval church. The necessity for an inner regeneration which led to rigorous outer discipline was substituted for the rituals which grew out of the doctrines of penance and the efficacy of the Mass. The Reformation, in its attempt to intensify and purify, thus emphasized different ideas in the complex of Christian thought. Central to the organization of Reformation thought is the conviction of human depravity. Left to his own devices, man must surely perish and be damned, for he is innately depraved, and the separation of nature and supernature is too great to be bridged by human institutional devices. What alleviates the human situation is the fact of God's grace and man's response through faith, but, since grace is external to man and results from God's will, there is a resultant emphasis upon predestination as opposed to "free will." Although the English Reformation tended to emphasize "election" rather than "reprobation," the fact of double predestination (the election of some and the rejection of others) is always implicit.[11] Within such a theological scheme it is possible for Wager to explore man's pilgrimage to hell-mouth.

Wager tends to hold in suspension our judgment of Moros and of his freedom. The Prologue announces that nothing can allure evil nature to good manners (ll. 44–46), but Exercitation argues that man falls willingly into vice (ll. 235–238), and failure is seemingly a result of choice. The virtues suspend their judgment and argue that it is a question of nurture rather than nature. Furthermore, Wager has constructed the play to create the illusion of choice, since he begins with the virtues and the opportunity of Moros to choose the discipline which leads to piety. From the beginning Moros possesses a spark of wit which redeems him from utter stupidity. He makes witty jokes at the expense of others, and he uses his wit to escape the beatings of Discipline. Yet as we watch the progression of folly, we recognize that such folly is doomed. The resolution of the action comes when God's Judgment urges Moros:

> If thou hast grace for mercy now call,
> Yet thy soul perchance thou mayst save;
> For his mercy is above his works all,
> On penitent sinners he is wont mercy to have.
> (ll. 1799–1802)

But there is no grace, and Moros interprets his mortal sickness in physical terms so that Confusion concludes: "Thy malice will not let

[11] C. H. and K. George, *The Protestant Mind of the English Reformation* (Princeton, 1961), Chap. 1; cf. W. A. Clebsch, *England's Earliest Protestants* (New Haven, 1964).

thee thy folly to see/ So that thou hast not the grace thy life to amend" (ll. 1837–1838). In the course of the play the spark of wit becomes malicious insolency and ultimately depravity, and at the end Moros stands revealed for what he has always been, a depraved fool. No amount of nurture could alter his nature.

The choice of a depraved hero has consequences for the development of the action, for there is little need for intrigue on the part of the forces of evil, and they need not seriously plot to capture Moros. Indeed, Wrath objects to the assumption of disguises as unnecessary. Although his objection is not totally valid because Moros does have some wit, however depraved, his objection allows us to accept the device of synonyms which extends the allegory. The role of the virtues is also diminished. That their arguments cannot convert Moros is made clear by Moros' asides. Ultimately they function to define the set of assumptions within which the play operates, and perhaps to qualify the pessimism of reprobation. Fortune and evil are finally contained within the framework of providential theory, for the devils are divine agents, and Fortune, if motivating the rise of Moros, is not responsible for his fall.

What disturbs the modern reader is the comedy of the play. As a fool the hero is clearly a source of laughter, and his antics precipitate farcical episodes. Our laughter at young Moros is one thing, but our laughter at old Moros (and there is laughter) is another, for if he is borne away on the back of Confusion, he is borne away to his damnation. We must recognize that there is always a serious undercurrent which qualifies the wit and the farce. The witty punning of Moros leads to blasphemy. The mode is perhaps alien to the twentieth century, which tends to resolve the ambivalence by suppressing either the comic or the tragic implications. Both are present, however, and both arise from the hero rather than from the vice. The grotesque humor of the play is perhaps in a direct descent from the judgment plays of the mystery cycles and looks ahead to the fortunes of Faustus.

In writing *Enough* for a larger company, Wager was able to avoid some of the technical difficulties and awkwardnesses which characterize *The Longer*. The larger cast allows Wager a greater flexibility in the use of alternation and suppression, and he can thus achieve a greater sense of movement. By developing two major characters, a protagonist and an antagonist, he defines the conflict more sharply. While the basic metaphor of the pilgrimage is retained, the metaphor is disguised and there is less sense of symbolic progression.

The presence of two heroes, Heavenly Man and Worldly Man, might suggest the alternation of two teams in a sequence of comic and serious scenes, but such an expectation is unfulfilled. Heavenly Man appears in the beginning of the opening sequence; after his meeting with Worldly Man, he appears only twice: first to deliver a twenty-line chorus which bridges sections one and two, and secondly in the final scene to receive his reward. Although he speaks of being tried in the "furnace of adversity" (l. 1494), there is no dramatic investigation of his suffering. Because he does not waver, there is no need for reintroduction by the virtues with whom he is associated. However limited his role, he does function to define one of the poles of the play, and as a result the final scene is less of an appendage than that of *The Longer*.

In terms of dramatic conflict, Wager realizes the potential of the depraved hero more fully in Worldly Man than in Moros. In *The Longer* the hero's folly is progressively exposed in scenes which are essentially exempla; in *Enough* the hero seems to create his own damnation by a series of actions. The difference is pointed up by a comparison of the opening speeches of the two heroes. When Moros sings "the foot of many songs," he is merely exemplifying his folly. The opening quatrain of Worldly Man's soliloquy suggests the obvious greed which characterizes him, but the remainder of the speech serves to define the ways in which worldliness operates and thus to prepare us for Worldly Man's actions. The second quatrain, with its prudence and its worldly wisdom, not only anticipates his defense against the arguments of Heavenly Man and Contentation, but also readies us for the particular attack which Covetous will make. The third quatrain, with its rationalizations which moralize greed, looks ahead to the treatment of the Tenant and the Hireling. Throughout, the soliloquy goes beyond mere exemplification. The overconfidence and greed of Worldly Man suggest the moral blindness of the hero who answers the ironic question "who can tell what his end shall be" with the assertion that he will have that "in respect and see." Thus, Wager presents a character who will generate conflict.

Moreover, the direct exposition of the opening soliloquy is translated into concrete action in the ironic conversion and subsequent fall of the hero. The defense of greed by the argument that imprudence can be wicked collapses suddenly before the arguments of Heavenly Man and Contentation. There is no interest here in the psychology of conversion but only in the dramatic expression of it. However faulty the conversion may seem to the twentieth century, the expressed willingness to reform is not a trick, as is Moros' attempt to escape a beating. Moreover, as Covetous argues, repentant sinners can obtain mercy. The conversion serves to establish the moral potentiality of Worldly Man. When he falls to Covetous' temptation, which is basically an appeal to prudence, Worldly Man falls through choice. If he errs from the blindness of his nature (cf. 1. 862, "It will not out of the flesh that is bred in the bone verily"), Worldly Man has had an opportunity to achieve salvation.

What remains is to illustrate the progressive hardening of the heart. Wager does so by giving two concrete episodes which are implicitly symbolic rather than explicitly allegorical. The interview with the Tenant and Hireling leads to a situation which echoes the Biblical parable of the barn-builder (Luke 12:16–20); and the Prophet, whose words inspire fear and who warns of the suddenness of judgment, is like a contemporary preacher. Who, indeed, can tell when his end shall be? Finally the death scene where Worldly Man is attended by his chaplain and physician brings the progression to the climax, for Worldly Man is concerned only with his possessions and thus merits his damnation. There is a tendency in the final sections to use concrete types rather than pure abstractions. It is only in the concluding dialogue that the play returns to "pure" allegory.

The introduction of an antagonist serves to clarify the conflict. The role of the vice, like that of Worldly Man, demands the full time of one actor. He is supported by a trio of subordinates who initiate the counter-action. The quartet disguise themselves, and the deception of Worldly Man involves fair-seeming evil. Although the trio of rogues is suppressed, Covetous remains on stage, and his role as Master Receiver is not a new role. The stabilizing of the vice helps to strengthen the episodic plot and to lessen the sense of symbolic progression.

Although the formulas of alternation and suppression are at work, the pattern of alternation is limited and the episodes less clearly marked. If the virtues and vices are juxtaposed, they also confront each other in the initial action. Moreover, the logic of plot grows out of the situation rather than being superimposed by the demands of the allegory. The introduction of Heavenly Man to bridge sections one and two is mechanical, but he does not provide external motivation as does Fortune in *The Longer*. The bridging of sections two and three is accomplished by retaining Worldly Man on stage so that the action flows directly into the judgment scene. The formula for suppression is also less rigidly followed. Among the virtues none are lost, and Rest is added as Heavenly Man's reward. Among the vices, the three rogues give way to the Tenant, Hireling, and Prophet who in turn are replaced by Ignorance, the Physician, and God's Plagues. Such a pattern of suppression does not emphasize the linear, symbolic progression which characterizes *The Longer*.

Though *The Longer* is allegorically not far removed from its medieval prototypes, *Enough* tends to narrow the focus of the allegory. Wager particularizes by replacing the traditional hero Mankind with Worldly Man and Heavenly Man, and by introducing types such as the Tenant and Hireling. Perhaps the popish priest Ignorance is an intermediate between the abstractions such as Covetous and the concrete types of the social satire. But whatever differences in allegoric method we may detect, the story of Worldly Man is made meaningful by the traditional symbolic mode. The bare stage may represent middle earth, but the presence of Satan and God's Plagues suggests the larger dimensions. Moreover, the costume changes define the career of Worldly Man and dramatize the fair-seeming quality of the vice.

The difference between the two plays lies less in the use of formulas or in the mode than in the tone. In *Enough* the comedy does not derive from Worldly Man. It is only the vices who indulge in comic interplay and in the farce of a mock battle. Covetous and Ignorance initiate broad comedy in the death scene, and there is ambivalence in our reactions. If Satan is funny, he remains Satan and the piggyback ride is to hell. The ambivalence is qualified partly because the Physician refuses to indulge in the comedy. Moreover, while in *The Longer* Moros is the center of the satire, in *Enough* the satire of the second section is spread more widely and played straight. The removal of the Worldly Man from the center of the comedy and the transference of the comedy to the vices tend to subordinate it to the tragedy.

Wager's achievement lies in his experimentation with the formulas of the moral interlude and in his contribution to "homilectic tragedy." It is perhaps too easy to dismiss the plays as crude efforts without recognizing the technical competence with which Wager handles the limitations of the Tudor stage. The moral play in the symbolic mode is alien to the realism of the twentieth century, but its strangeness should not obscure its effectiveness in its own terms. In Wager's plays we sense the larger dimensions of the tragic world, for the hero is defeated by forces which are greater than he and the violation of order leads inevitably to retribution. The plays reflect the *de casibus* tradition as it was modified in *The Mirror for Magistrates* where, if Fortune's wheel is the dominant metaphor for the fall not only of princes but of men like Jack Cade, sin is the causative factor. Interestingly, although Fortune motivates the rise of Moros, she does not cause his fall; and the motif disappears in *Enough* where the emphasis is thrown upon sin. Previously both *Nice Wanton* and *Trial of Treasure* had presented defeat; but neither play focused so clearly on the defeat of the hero, and neither play presented the enigmas of tragedy which arise out of the conflict between determinism and free will. If Wager relies implicitly upon Reformation theology to suggest the predestined reprobation of his heroes, he nevertheless presents them as capable of freely working out their own salvation. Although the potentiality for good is questionable in the case of Moros and limited in the case of Worldly Man, the illusion of the possibility of repentance and thus of salvation is maintained. We do accept their responsibility for their fortunes even though there is little expectation of a change in Moros, and even though the suddenness of death denies Worldly Man the chance to repent. Given the limitations of the moral interlude, Wager attempts to portray the possibility of failure within the context of Christianity. For Wager and for the Reformation the fact of reprobation was a tragic possibility.

THE TEXT

Only single copies of the original quartos survive, *The Longer* in the British Museum, *Enough* in the Huntington Library. Photostats of these have served as the basis for the present text. Neither play was reprinted in the sixteenth or seventeenth century. Brandl's reprint of *The Longer* in the *Shakespeare Jahrbuch*, XXXVI (1900), is the only modern edition of that play and has been collated with the present text. A facsimile text of *The Longer* was made by J. S. Farmer (*Old English Plays, Student's Facsimile Edition*, 1910), of *Enough* by S. de Ricci (Huntington Reprints, 1920).

The two quartos pose no bibliographical problems. *The Longer* has as its running title "A nevv Commedie, called/ The longer thou liuest the more foole thou art" (lenger on A4; fole on C3). It has no colophon but prints on G4^v a double-headed eagle device which presumably represents Richard Jones' shop, the Spread Eagle in Fleet Lane. There are twenty-eight unnumbered leaves using black letter with roman for incidental purposes. Speech prefixes are in roman, and from sig. B1 on, a smaller type is used. The collation is as follows: A–G4 (misprinting G3 as A3); A1 Title, A1^v The Players Names, A2 Prologue, A3–G4^r Text. The running title for *Enough* is "Inough is as good as a feast." There are twenty-six unnumbered leaves using black letter with roman for incidental purposes. The running title, "Finis" to the Prologue, and the initial stage direction are in italic. The collation is: A–F4–G2; A1 Title (v blank), A2 Prologue, A3–G2^v Text.

Although the plays may have been written for a particular troupe, there is no evidence to suggest that the text of either play is related to a theatrical promptbook. Speech prefixes are seemingly authorial and tend to be sparsely descriptive. If entrances are not always indicated and exits occasionally omitted, stage business is normally noted. In *The Longer*, although exits are in the right-hand margin, speech prefixes and stage directions are in the left margin and entrances are often combined with speech prefixes. The position of stage directions to the left of the text probably originates in the printing house and does not here indicate prompt copy. In *Enough* speech prefixes are centered and stage directions are normally printed in the right margin.

The manuscript for each play seems to have been clear, for the compositor had little difficulty with his copy. Brandl notes the omission of several lines in *The Longer*, and there are at least two places in *Enough* where violation of the rhyme scheme may indicate that lines have been dropped. If so, the errors probably originated with the compositor rather than from the copy. Errors in the text are often the result of foul case or of broken type. No attempt has been made to record misspacings, which occur frequently.

The modernization of the text tends to obscure the rhyme scheme. Both plays use couplets, quatrains and rhyme royal. To meet the requirements of rhyme, Wager uses many dialectal or older forms. Occasionally the compositor had difficulty with northern forms, e.g., *The Longer*, l. 148, "boll" for "bow," which the compositor sets as "boule," perhaps mistaking it for a variant form of "bowl." Unless otherwise noted all definitions are from the *OED*. When Wager paraphrases the Latin quotations in the text, they have not been translated in the footnotes. The source of the quotations is indicated whenever possible, but many remain unrecognized. Where necessary, the Latin of the quotations has been regularized and the changes duly noted.

This edition was made possible by a fellowship grant from the Folger Shakespeare Library; many thanks are due to the staff and especially to Miss Dorothy Mason and Miss Virginia La Marr. Thanks are also due to Colby College for a grant from its faculty research funds. Permission has been graciously given by the Huntington Library, San Marino, California, to reprint their copy of *Enough Is as Good as a Feast* and by the British Museum, to reprint their copy of *The Longer Thou Livest*.

R. Mark Benbow

Colby College

THE LONGER THOU LIVEST

THE PLAYERS' NAMES

PROLOGUE	FORTUNE	
MOROS	IGNORANCE	
DISCIPLINE	CRUELTY	
PIETY	IMPIETY	5
EXERCITATION	PEOPLE	
IDLENESS	GOD'S JUDGMENT	
INCONTINENCE	CONFUSION	
WRATH		

Four may play it easily   10

PROLOGUE
EXERCITATION
WRATH [*alias* MANHOOD]   } *for one*
CRUELTY [*alias* PRUDENCE]
GOD'S JUDGMENT   15

MOROS   } *for another*
FORTUNE

DISCIPLINE
INCONTINENCE [*alias* PLEASURE] } *for another*   20
IMPIETY [*alias* PHILOSOPHY]
CONFUSION

PIETY
IDLENESS [*alias* PASTIME] } *for another*   25
IGNORANCE [*alias* ANTIQUITY]
PEOPLE

---

3. *Moros*] The name is derived from the Latin deponent verb "moror," meaning "to be a fool."

6. *Exercitation*] exercise, practice or training; here in the sense of vocation (cf. ll. 1903 ff.).

8. *Incontinence*] lust, but also inconstancy (cf. ll. 622–623 and 632–635).

23. *Confusion*] The words "the devilles messenger" in a late sixteenth-century hand appear opposite the name "Confusion" in the list of characters. Craik points out (p. 132) that Confusion is a name given to a devil in S. Robinson's *The Reward of Wickedness* (1574) and that Wager's use of the character may be traditional.

A Very Merry and Pithy Comedy Called
The Longer Thou Livest
The More Fool Thou Art

THE PROLOGUE

Aristophanes, as Valerius doth tell,
Introduceth Pericles in a comedy
That he, being reduced again out of hell
Unto th'Athenienses, did thus prophesy:
Bring up no lions in your cities wantonly,   5
For, as you bring them up in acts pernicious,
So in the same you must be to them obsequious.
By this, saith Valerius, he doth admonish
That rich men's sons be from evil manners refrained
Lest that with profuse fondness we do them nourish   10
(Virtue of them ever after be disdained)
So that, when authority they have obtained,
They themselves being given to inconvenience
Oppress their subjects under their obedience.
O how noble a thing is good education,   15
For all estates profitable, but for them chiefly
Which by birth are like to have gubernation
In public weals, that they may rule ever justly;

4. th'Athenienses,] *this edn.*; Tha-   9. men's] *this edn.*; men *Q, Brandl.*
thenienses *Q, Brandl.*

---

1. *Valerius*] Wager translates fairly closely a passage in Valerius Maxi-
mus' *De factorum dictorum quoque memorabilium exemplis.*
3. *reduced*] used in its Latin meaning "brought back."
4. *Athenienses*] Athenians; Wager perhaps borrows the Latin form from
Valerius.
7. *in the same*] i.e., pernicious acts.
13. *inconvenience*] impropriety.
17. *gubernation*] government.

For while the Romans did foresee this matter wisely,
They had a wise senate which prevailed alway,   20
And that being neglected, they fell soon to decay.
To be a good man it is also expedient
Of good parents to be begotten and born;
Indeed to all men it is most evident
That a pleasant rose springeth of a sharp thorn,   25
But commonly of good seed proceedeth good corn.
Good parents in good manners do instruct their child,
Correcting him when he beginneth to grow wild.
The bringing up of a child from his tender age
In virtue is a great help to be an honest man;   30
But when youth is suffer'd to have his own rage,
It falleth to much calamity now and then.
I would wish parents and masters to do what they can
Both to teach and correct their youth with reason,
That it may profit the public weal another season.   35
To help hereto good schoolmasters are necessary—
Sage, sober, expert, learned, gentle and prudent—
Under such masters youth can never miscarry;
For either they refrain evils with good advisement,
Or to occupy the mind good lessons do invent.   40
To youth nothing in the world is so pernicious
As to be conversant with masters lascivious.
Bringing up is a great thing, so is diligence,
But nothing, God except, is so strong as nature;
For neither counsel, learning nor sapience   45
Can an evil nature to honest manners allure.
Do we not see at these days so many past cure

44. as] *Brandl*; of *Q*.

---

25. *rose . . . thorn*] Tilley, R 179.
31. *rage*] violent desire, will.
32. *then*] In the sixteenth century "than" and "then" were not distinguished in either spelling or pronunciation. Here as elsewhere, rhymes may be accurate although dependent upon phonetic shifts or dialectal pronunciation; cf. H. C. Wyld, *Studies in English Rhymes from Surrey to Pope* (London, 1923).
39. *refrain*] restrain.
43–49.] Behind these lines lies the Reformation emphasis upon the doctrine of human depravity.

That nothing can their crookedness rectify
Till they have destroyed them utterly?
The image of such persons we shall introduce,   50
Represented by one whom Moros we do call;
By him we shall declare the unthrifty abuse
Of such as had lever to folly and idleness fall
Than to harken to sapience when he doth call,
Their process, how their whole life they do spend,   55
And what shame they come to at the last end.
Wherefore this our matter we entitle and name:
The longer thou livest, the more fool thou art.
Are there not many which do verify the same?
Yes, I warrant you, and naturally play that part,   60
Yea, even from the judgment seat unto the cart.
But truly we mean no person particularly,
But only to specify of such generally.
Wholesome lessons now and then we shall interlace,
Good for the ignorant, not hurtful to the wise;   65
Honest mirth shall come in and appear in place,
Not to th'advancement but to the shame of vice.
To extol virtue without fail is our device.
A season we shall desire you of patience,
And to make you merry we will do our diligence.   70

Here enter'th Moros, *counterfeiting a vain gesture and a foolish countenance
[and] singing the foot of many songs as fools were wont [, and* Discipline].

MOROS.

    Broom, broom on hill,

59. verify] verefie *Q*; vereste *Brandl.*   70–70.1 diligence./ *Here*] *this edn.*;
67. th'advancement] *this edn.*; tha-   dilligence./ FINIS./ ¶ Here *Q*,
duauncement *Q*, *Brandl.*   *Brandl.*

   48. *rectify*] make straight.   49. *them*] i.e., themselves.
   53. *lever*] rather.
   61. *from . . . cart*] Although the phrase may be merely an inclusive
description (from judge to criminal), it may also describe Moros' progress
from pre-eminence to damnation.
   63. *specify*] exhibit.
   66. *in place*] "in its place"; perhaps also the acting space from the Latin
"platea."
   70.2 *foot*] the refrain of a song.
   71–99.] The songs Moros sings were popular tunes or nursery rhymes.
Robert Laneham reports (1575) that in Captain Cox's collection of books

The gentle broom on hive hill,
Broom, broom on hive hill,
The gentle broom on hive hill.
The broom stands on hive hill-a.   75

Robin, lend to me thy bow; thy bow;
Robin, the bow; Robin lend to me thy bow-a.

There was a maid came out of Kent,
Dainty love, dainty love;
There was a maid came out of Kent,   80
Dangerous be.
There was a maid came out of Kent,
Fair, proper, small and gent,
As ever upon the ground went,
For so should it be.   85

By a bank as I lay, I lay,
Musing on things past, hey how.

Tom-a-lin and his wife and his wife's mother,
They went over a bridge all three together;
The bridge was broken and they fell in.   90
The devil go with all, quoth Tom-a-lin.

Martin Swart and his man, sodledum, sodledum,
Martin Swart and his man, sodledum bell.

Come over the bourn, Bessie,
My little pretty Bessie,   95
Come over the bourn, Bessie, to me.

The white dove sat on the castle wall,

---

72. hive] *this edn.*; hill Q, *Brandl.*   81. Dangerous] *Brandl*; Daungersus
78. came] *this edn.*; come Q, *Brandl.*   Q.

---

were the following "ballets and songs, all auncient; az Broom broom on
Hil; So Wo iz me begon, troly lo; Over a Whinny Meg; Hey ding a ding;
Bony lass upon a Green. My bony on[e] gave me a bek; By a bank az I
lay . . ." (*Robert Laneham's Letter*, in John Nichols, *The Progresses and Public
Processions of Queen Elizabeth* [London, 1823], I, 454); see Chappell and
Wooldridge, *Old English Popular Music* (London, 1893) and J. Ritson, *Ancient Songs and Ballads* (London, 1829) for versions of tunes.
  83. *gent*] graceful, pretty.

I bend my bow and shoot her I shall,
I put her in my glove, both feathers and all.

I laid my bridle upon the shelf   100
If you will any more, sing it yourself.

DISCIPLINE.

O Lord, are you not ashamed
Thus vainly the time to spend?
Your friends by you are defamed.
I would have you this gear to amend.   105
What? to a good age now you grow;
It is time childishness to forsake.
I would find somewhat to do, I trow,
And not like a fool such a noise to make,
Going up and down like a witless boy,   110
Singing and bellowing like a daw.
If you will not amend this toy,
We will bring you to another awe.

MOROS.

I have twenty moe songs yet.
A fond woman to my mother,   115
As I war wont in her lap to sit,
She taught me these and many other.
I can sing a song of Robin Redbreast
And my little pretty nightingale—
There dwelleth a jolly foster here by west—   120
Also, I come to drink some of your Christmas ale.
When I walk by myself alone,
It doth me good my songs to render;

---

105. *gear*] business.   111. *daw*] jackdaw.
113. *awe*] fear, restraint.
114. *moe*] more.
115. *fond woman to*] *to* is used in the sense of possession; i.e., "my mother's foolish servant."
116. *war*] subjunctive plural.
118–121.] The following songs are not easily identifiable but may be nursery rhymes. As Brandl points out (p. 10), it is not clear in ll. 118–119 whether we have one or two songs; cf. I. and P. Opie, *The Oxford Dictionary of Nursery Rhymes* (Oxford, 1952), for rhymes concerning Robin Redbreast.
120. *foster*] forester.
123. *It doth me good*] it pleases me.

Such pretty things would soon be gone,
If I should not sometime them remember.   125

DISCIPLINE.

Gaudet stultis natura creandis
(Nature hath a pleasure fools to create)
Ut malvis atque urticis et vilibus herbis
(As mallows, nettles, and weeds of that rate)
Hii sunt obtuso ingenio crasso cerebro   130
(These are dull of wit and of a gross brain)
Et nihili pendunt animi bona depeci ludo
(And set at nought virtue, given to pastime vain).
These verses I may on you verify
Except you will take another way;   135
I would be glad your manners to rectify.
If you would hear what I will say.
For shame, I say yet again;
Forget your babish vanity;
Folly and vice you must refrain   140
And give yourself to humanity.

MOROS.

I am good at scourging of my top;
You would laugh to see me mossell the peg.
Upon my one foot prettily I can hop
And dance trimly about an egg.   145
Also when we play and hunt the fox,
I outrun all the boys in the school.

126–133.] Discipline is a model teacher who translates each verse as he
goes along. Latin tags which are translated in text are not glossed.
    129. *mallows*] any one of the family of plants which includes hollyhocks
and okra; here, a weed.
    134. *verify*] ascertain the truth by comparison.
    139. *babish*] babyish.
    143. *mossell the peg*] mumble-the-peg. The unsuccessful player is com-
pelled to draw out of the ground with his teeth a peg which the others
have driven in. "Mossell" is an obsolete form of "morsel" which Florio
(*A World of Words*, edn. 1598) gives as a synonym of "bite" (*s.v.* "Mor-
secchiare"); the phrase means "bite the peg" which is also the meaning
of "mumble-the-peg."
    146. *hunt the fox*] In the game one boy is permitted to run out a certain
distance before the others pursue him to catch him before he returns to
home base.

My mother gave me a boll of box;
Alone I am to handle such a tool.
I can come softly behind a boy   150
And give him a blow and run away.
My mother teacheth me many a pretty toy;
You shall know what they be one day.
When to fight, quoth my father, thou dost purpose,
Pluck him upward by the hair still,   155
With thy knuckles strike him on the nose.
Let him not go till thou have thy will.

DISCIPLINE.

Quales quisque sibi natos eduxit habebit;
As one bringeth up his children, saith he,
So shall he have them, wise or without wit.   160
Therefore, parents are to blame as here we see.
But to you now, I pray you tell,
Be these the best lessons of your parents?

MOROS.

No forsooth, I can ring the saunce bell
And fetch fire when they go to matins.   165

DISCIPLINE.

Better it were to have no education
Than to be instructed in any part of idolatry;
For there is no part without abomination
But altogether full of sects and heresy.

MOROS.

Nay, I can more than that. Hark in your ear: 170
"To call him knave"—I go not behind the door—
"Be bold," quoth my father, "and do not fear;

148. boll] *this edn.*; Boule *Q*,   161. see] *Brandl*; ses *Q*.
Brandl.

---

148. *boll of box*] bow of boxwood; the quarto spelling "boule" suggests
that *boll*, a Scotch form of "bow," was mistaken for a variant spelling of
"bowl."

164. *saunce*] Sanctus bell which was the bell rung at the singing of the
Sanctus in the Mass; for the Reformation this was a popish superstition
and led to idolatry since the ringing of the bell was a signal to genuflect
(cf. ll. 166–169).

165. *matins*] properly the midnight office but often sung at dawn; Moros
carries coals to keep warm.

If thy mother anger thee, call her whore."

DISCIPLINE.

Without doubt such lewd persons there are,
And this is the cause that so many evil men   175
Now replenish the earth with sorrow and care,
Not one good man is scarcely among ten.
Let this ungracious and foolish person
Be as an image of such bringing up,
Like to be as unhappy a patron   180
As ever drank of any man's cup.
For the love that we owe to mankind,
And chiefly unto Christianity,
We will prove to alter his mind
And bring him to humanity.   185

[*Enter* Piety.]

PIETY.

All hail, right honorable Discipline.
Well-occupied evermore I do you find,
Instructing one or other with doctrine
According to your natural kind,
Which is both comely manners to teach   190
And also to minister correction.
If all men unto your precepts would reach,
Soon should be cleansed all infection.

DISCIPLINE.

O welcome Piety, the door of all virtue.
If you consisteth God's honor, virtue and love,   195
Without the which no good thing can ensue,
As by the Christian poet we do prove:
Hoc sine virtutis alias nihil est putato,
Without the worship of God omnipotent
(Which learned men properly call piety)   200
Other virtues, be they never so excellent,
Are esteemed but as things of vility.

---

178. *ungracious*] unmannerly, but also graceless in a theological sense.
180. *patron*] example.
184. *prove*] try.
202. *vility*] vileness.

Enter Exercitation.

EXERCITATION.

　　And as virtue is no virtue without Piety
　　So, without the same, vice cannot be eschewed.
　　Piety is a true honor of God's majesty　　　　　　　　205
　　Wherewith Christians should be endued.
　　God to worship, to love, to fear, to praise,
　　His holy commandments to obey,
　　To be occupied in his laws nights and days—
　　This properly is called Piety, I say.　　　　　　　　210

MOROS.

　　By my troth, if you will can me good thank,
　　I will bring you to a pretty bird's nest.
　　Verily, I think it be a red shank;
　　She is white in the tail and black in the breast.

DISCIPLINE.

　　The longer thou livest the more fool thou art,　　　　215
　　The more instruction, the less sapience;
　　Grace will not enter into a foolish heart,
　　Iniquity stoppeth out intelligence
　　To you, Piety and Exercitation.
　　Of such folly I have admonished him;　　　　　　　　220
　　But I can have none other communication,
　　So vainly have his parents nourished him.

PIETY.

　　Thus, the Christian poet to write was wont:
　　Without industry, all things mortal—
　　Naturae instinctu, sponte ruunt—　　　　　　　　　225
　　By very nature unto vice do fall.
　　But as we see by experience
　　A barren field is made fat and fertile
　　If men will adhibit their diligence

225. *instinctu*] *Brandl*; inscinctu *Q*.

---

205. *honor*] esteem.
211. *can . . . thank*] say thank you, express gratitude.
218. *stoppeth out*] excludes.
219. *To*] concerning, about.
228. *fat*] rich, fertile.
229. *adhibit*] employ.

And labor about it awhile;   230
So though this young fellow be foolish as yet,
With labor and diligent admonition
He may, in process of time, learn wit
And be willing to take erudition.

EXERCITATION.

Virtue hath very hard entrances,   235
But ready is the way unto vice;
And thereto fall we all, not by chances,
But willingly if we be not ware and wise.
Now whereas the lad's education
Hath been rude, foolish, fond, and vain,   240
Let us give him good information
And to profit him let us gladly take pain.
Discipline, do you still your endeavor
To cause him perfectly to know Piety—
That is, God to serve, to fear, to love, to honor—   245
And his parents to obey with humility.
Then you know that I, Exercitation,
According as I shall see his aptness,
I will exercise him in good occupation
Whereby he shall eschew Idleness.   250

MOROS.

In Saint Nicholas' shambles there is enough,
Or in Eastcheape or at Saint Katherine's;
There be good puddings at the sign of the plow,
You never did eat better sauserlings.

---

243. *do*] carry out.
243. *still*] always.
251–254.] The Butchers' Hall was located near the parish church of St.
Nicholas in the Grey Friars area of London when there was a meat market;
shambles was the name for the stalls for the sale of meat. There was another
meat market in Eastcheape in Pudding Lane where the butchers made
sausages, known as "puddings" or *sauserlings*. St. Katherine's was an area
known for its brew houses (Stow, I, 210–211, 216, 316). In 1586 there was
a tenement in the parish of St. Mary Woolchurch called "the sign de la
Ploughe" (*London Inquisitions Post-Mortem* [London, 1908], III, 88); and
Wager's reference may be a topical allusion.
251.] Moros interprets Piety's command to *eschew Idleness* to mean "to
avoid addleness (putrification, especially applied to eggs)"; he then
develops the pun on "chew" by referring to eating wholesome food.

–13–

DISCIPLINE.

This folly is not his innocency,   255
Which can in this wise lewdly overwhart,
But it is a malicious insolency
Which proceedeth from a wicked heart.

PIETY.

Come hither, brother, come hither;
Your name to me you must disclose.   260

DISCIPLINE.

His folly his master did consider,
And therefore called him nothing but Moros.

PIETY.

Moros is a fool by interpretation,
But wisdom goeth not all by the name;
He that is a fool in conversation,   265
As a fool in deed we may him blame.
I know some that be named happy,
And some good, blessed, and fortunable;
Yet truly there be none more unlucky,
Worse, more wicked and unprofitable.   270
And though "Moros" a fool doth signify,
Yet you may be wise, as I trust you will
If you will serve God as you ought diligently;
He shall give you wisdom, if you pray still.

MOROS.

I may tell you, my father did like me well,   275
I am the wisest child that ever he had.
Often times I have heard him say or tell,
"My boy Moros will prove a wise lad."

EXERCITATION.

If you can remember your father's saying,
Why can you not remember good lessons as well?   280
You may not set your mind upon playing,

257. insolency] *this edn.*; insolentie   270. unprofitable] *Brandl*; vnprof-
Q, Brandl (*perhaps reflecting Latin*   fitabe *Q*.
"*insolentia*").

255. *innocency*] simplicity, childishness.
256. *lewdly*] ignorantly as well as immorally.
256. *overwhart*] hinder or pervert; dialectal form of "overthwart."

−14−

But apply yourself to Discipline's counsel.

DISCIPLINE.

My counsel is that you fear God above all;
Pray unto him to give you sapience;
Cease not upon his holy name to call.   285
Be meek in sprite, fast and keep abstinence;
His ministers (priests and preachers
Such as rule the holy church catholic)
Obey, I mean such as be true teachers.
Company not with any heretic.   290
An heretic him holy doctors do call
Which erreth in God's most sacred scripture,
Which is blind and seeth not his own fall,
But maliciously doth in error endure.
The greatest heresy that ever was   295
Hath the pope and his adherents published,
Yea, the heresy of Arius it doth pass,
For Christ and his benefits it hath extinguished.
Example by the wicked Mass satisfactory
Which to Christ's death they make equivalent,   300
For they call it a sacrifice propitiatory,
Which is an heresy most pestilent;
Again, prayer to saints that be dead,
Which is a great point of infidelity,
For they forsake Christ which is the head   305
Who taught to worship in sprite and verity.

EXERCITATION.

Can you recite wisely again
Discipline's counsel and monition?

MOROS.

Can I? yea, I trow I can and that plain
If you suffer me without interruption.   310

---

286. *sprite*] spirit.

297. *Arius*] Greek theologian (d. 356 A.D.) who argued that Christ was
not the eternal Son of God nor of the same substance.

299. *Mass satisfactory*] The Protestant Reformation denied that the Mass
itself was sufficient to achieve salvation and thus denied the validity of the
trental masses (series of thirty intercessory masses) said for the dead by
Chantry priests in order to shorten the period in Purgatory.

First, he said, bear an odd end with an all,
Play now and then in thy master's absence,
Cease not a knave by his right name to call,
Much on the spit is past abstinence.

DISCIPLINE.

Lo you hear? what a patron this is.   315
Think you that he is not past grace?

EXERCITATION.

Yet I say, he that hath wit to do this,
May turn to virtue also in space.

PIETY.

Come hither. I pray thee tell me but one thing,
How intendest thou to live another day?   320

MOROS.

How? truly, make merry, dance and sing,
Set cock-a-hoop and play care away.

PIETY.

Seeing that you have none other respect
But your life's days in folly to spend,
Discipline must you now and then correct.   325
That unto wisdom you may yourself bend.

MOROS.

Correct, quoth he? why, shall I be beaten?
My father will not suffer that, I trow.

DISCIPLINE.

You begin to be scabby and worm-eaten;
It is time salt upon you to strow.   330
Sirrah, do you see what I have here?
The wise man willeth an ass to have a scourge;
You have learned folly many a year,

324. life's] *this edn.*; life *Q, Brandl.*

311–314.] Moros' reply is a witty perversion of Discipline's instructions
(ll. 283–286); the wit arises from the similarity of word or phrase which
converts piety into blasphemy.

320. *another day*] Moros interprets this in temporal terms but Piety is
referring to the life to come.

322. *cock-a-hoop*] to turn on the tap and let the liquor flow; hence, to
abandon oneself to reckless enjoyment.

330. *salt . . . to strow*] to season; i.e., to beat.

From the same now I must you purge.
You that have the wit to mock and to scorn,   335
What wit you have to wisdom I will see.
Upon your sides this scourge shall be worn
Except you will speak rightly after me:
I will love and fear God above all.

MOROS (*say after him*).

I will love and fear God above all.   340

DISCIPLINE.

He might vouchsafe to give me sapience.

MOROS.

He might vouchsafe to give me sapience.

DISCIPLINE.

I shall not cease on his holy name to call.

MOROS.

I shall not cease on his holy name to call.

DISCIPLINE.

That he will open mine intelligence.   345

MOROS.

That he will open mine intelligence.

DISCIPLINE.

Well said.

MOROS.   Well said.

DISCIPLINE.

Say the same verses alone together
Like as you said them after me.

MOROS.

Say the same verses alone together   350
Like as you said them after me.

PIETY.

His meaning you do not consider;
Alone you must say the verses as they be.

MOROS.

His meaning you do not consider;

340.S.D.] *Q prints in left margin.*
340. I . . . all.] *this edn.*; I will loue
&c. *Q, Brandl.*
342. He . . . sapience.] *this edn.*; He
might vouchsafe &c. *Q, Brandl.*

344. I . . . call.] *this edn.*; I shall
not cease &c. *Q, Brandl.*
346. That . . . intelligence.] *this edn.*;
That he will &c. *Q, Brandl.*

Alone you must say the verses as they be.   355
EXERCITATION.
    You may say no more as he did say.
    He did but teach you your words wisely to frame.
MOROS.
    You may say no more as he did say.
    He did but teach you your words wisely to frame.
DISCIPLINE.
    With an ungracious fool we spend the day;   360
    He turneth all to a mock and a game.
MOROS.
    With an ungracious fool we spend the day;
    He turneth all to a mock and a game.
DISCIPLINE.
    Vexation, they say, giveth intelligence;
    Another while I will prove you with my scourge.   365
MOROS.
    Vexation, they say, giveth intelligence;
    Another while I will prove you with my scourge.
PIETY.
    This heady foolishness and negligence
    With correction away we must purge.
MOROS.
    This heady foolishness and negligence   370
    With correction away we must purge.
EXERCITATION.
    We will hold him while you do him beat.
    Lay on, Discipline, and do not spare.
MOROS.
    I trow I shall make you all three to sweat.
    Come one for one, and for you all I do not care.   375

                    Hold him and beat him.

    Body of God! alas, my arse, out! out! no more.
    Cry you mercy, a vengeance take you!

375.1.] *Q prints in margin to the left of
ll. 375–376.*

————————————————————————

    365. *while*] time.
    375. *Come one for one*] come one at a time.

                        –18–

For God's sake leave, mine arse is sore.
I will say as you will have me say now.

DISCIPLINE.

Say thus.

MOROS.   Say thus.   380

DISCIPLINE.

I will love and fear God above all
He might vouchsafe to give me sapience;
I will not cease on his holy name to call
That he may open mine intelligence.

PIETY.

Good son, say these words and think the same;   385
And we will teach you other good lessons moe.

MOROS.

You have put me out, God give you shame.
I wot not which way the devil they go.

DISCIPLINE (*repeat them again*).

I will love and fear God above all
He might vouchsafe to give me sapience;   390
I will not cease on his holy name to call
That he may open mine intelligence.

MOROS.

I will love porridge, when they be sod, beef and all;
For mutton good sauce is salt and onions.
Up unto the high dish when my dame they call,   395
While she openeth the pie, I pick the pinions.

PIETY.

Let us lose no more labor about this fool,
For the more he is taught the worse he is.

DISCIPLINE.

Hold him, and I will teach him a new school.

389–392. I . . . intelligence.]   *this*   *included within the line rather than*
edn.; Repete them againe: I will   *placed in the margin.*)
loue &c. *Q, Brandl.* (*The S.D. is*

---

378. *leave*] leave off, stop.
381–382.] elliptic construction parallel to ll. 383–384; "I will love . . .
that he . . . ."
393. *sod*] boiled.
395. *high dish*] the dish on the high or raised table in the hall.
396. *pinions*] wings.

He can speak the right that can speak this.   400

MOROS.

O beat me no more, I pray you heartily;
To make you to laugh I turned them this way.
Sometime I love to talk and sing merrily,
But I think no harm then, by this day.

EXERCITATION.

In you let us some towardness see,   405
For to make you a man we do intend.
To laugh, to be merry, to sing, times there be;
But in such things now we have no time to spend.

PIETY.

Let us hear how Discipline you do understand;
The sentence that he hath taught you, do you say.   410

MOROS [aside].

That is the best way, I think, to escape your hand,
But I trust to be even with you one day.—
I will love and fear God above all
He might vouchsafe to give me sapience;
I will not cease on his holy name to call   415
That he may open mine intelligence.

DISCIPLINE.

This is well if it be spoken with the heart;
Fear sometime causeth dissimulation.

MOROS.

I cannot speak it, I suppose, without a heart;
After fear cometh alway consolation.   420

PIETY.

I perceive that you have wit competently
If you would apply it unto virtue.
We will instruct you sufficiently
If our doctrine you will humbly ensue.

EXERCITATION.

By us you shall have this commodity: 425
In this life you shall be in reputation,
After this life you shall have felicity,
That is joy in the heavenly habitation.

---

405. *towardness*] disposition, readiness.
424. *ensue*] pursue.

DISCIPLINE.

My son, this order with you we will take.
First, I will commit you unto Piety,   430
Who the true servant of God shall you make,
And teach you to honor his Majesty,

Here let Moros *between every sentence say, "Gay gear," "good stuff," "very*
well," "fin-ado," with such mockish terms.

To love him, to pray to him, day and night;
To know his son Jesus Christ, our Lord,
Equal with the father in substance and might;   435
The Holy Ghost, the author of love and concord.
In him you shall learn God's word to hear,
Your duty to the ministers of the same,
Who the mysteries of God in their hearts do bear,
To esteem the sacraments each one by name.   440
Piety will teach you your duty to kings,
To rulers and magistrates in their degree,
Unto whom you must be obedient in all things
Concerning the statutes and laws of the country.
It is piety your parents to obey,   445
Yea, your prince and country to defend,
The poor to comfort ever as you may,
For the truth's sake your blood to spend.

MOROS.

Nay, ho there! By God, all things save blood.
He that breaketh my head, I will break his again.   450

PIETY.

Your understanding in that is not good;
Such appetites you must always refrain.

EXERCITATION.

After that you are endued with piety,
In me you shall have exercitation
To your own and other men's utility,   455
I mean a science or occupation

434. our Lord,] *Brandl; not in Q.*

---

440. *sacraments*] for Reformation Protestantism, baptism and holy
communion.
449. *ho*] hold, stop.

Which to learn do your diligence
And, being learned, do the same occupy
And, occupied, by experience
Seek to exercise them busily.   460

DISCIPLINE.

How say you? Will you dwell with Piety
And learn his instructions with a good will?

MOROS.

I thank you for your good mind toward me;
I will never go from you but dwell with you still.

PIETY.

First, unto you a testament here I give   465
Wherein you shall learn what the will of God is,
To pray upon and to learn your Christian beleve
And to amend your manners that be amiss.

MOROS.

God's santy, this is a goodly book indeed.
Be there any saints in it and pilcrows?   470
Ah sir, I have spied "Christ's cross me speed."
I may tell you I am past all my crossrows,
I have learned beyond the ten commandments.
Two years ago, doubtless, I was past grace;

465.] The book given to Moros is apparently some version of *The ABC with the Little Catechism* or *The ABC with the Catechism*. These volumes included the alphabet (crossrow), the ten commandments, graces (prayers), and the creed. The books were used in petty schools as the first readers; cf. T. W. Baldwin, *William Shakespeare's Petty School* (Urbana, Ill., 1943), Chap. 2.

467. *beleve*] belief, often used for the Apostles' Creed. The rhyme with *give* (l. 465) is possible; Levins (*Manipulus Vocabularum, A Dictionary of English and Latin Words*, edn. 1570) equates "give" with "grieve" and "sleeve" (*OED*, give^v (note on Morphology)).

469. *God's santy*] probably a corruption of "God's sanctity."

470. *saints*] Moros is looking for the woodcuts which decorated Catholic Primers and Hours of the Virgin Mary.

470. *pilcrows*] a mark (usually ¶) for a paragraph or for calling attention to specific matter.

471. *Christ's . . . speed*] In printing the alphabet, it was preceded by a cross, and the alphabet was thus known as a crossrow. The phrase *Christ's cross me speed* was the formula said before repeating the alphabet (cf. l. 1842).

474. *grace*] While the reference here is to having gone beyond the prayers, the word suggests a pun, for Moros is indeed beyond grace, salvation.

I am in the midst of God's judgments.   475
I trust to be as wise as he within short space.

PIETY.

I must have all these vain words to cease;
Another leaf you must turn now truly.

MOROS.

Of good milk if you will give me daily a mess,
You shall see I will wait upon you duly.   480

PIETY.

It is so that I may no longer tarry here;
I must go hence. Come, will you go with me?

MOROS.

Yea, that I will, for here is little good cheer;
What good fare you have, I purpose to see.

DISCIPLINE.

Look that you do yourself honestly behave,   485
For I purpose to see you every day thrice.
Neither mocks nor gauds shall your skin save;
I advise you therefore to be honest and wise.

EXERCITATION.

In doing well, fear ye no punishment;
Be ruled by the counsel of Discipline.   490
Your own folly will be your detriment
If you from Piety chance to decline.

MOROS.

I warrant you in pain of twenty shames
I am won now, you shall see me very honest;
But yer I go, yet let me know your names.   495
Declare them, I pray you, at my request.

DISCIPLINE.

You know that my name is Discipline.

---

475. *judgments*] Probably a reference to the doctrines of the Catechism,
although the Biblical distinction between "commandments" (direct com-
mands) and "judgments" (decisions of law courts) may be reflected here
(Exodus 20:6 and 21:1).

479. *mess*] portion.

487. *gauds*] tricks.

491. *detriment*] that which causes a loss.

495. *yer*] ere.

MOROS [*aside*].

    Very well, very well, Diricke Quintine.

    You are Master Diricke Quintine.

PIETY.

    Ofttimes you have heard me called Piety.   500

MOROS [*aside*].

    Master Pine-nut-tree and Master Diricke Quintine.

EXERCITATION.

    I exercise men in good works and doctrine,

    And therefore Exercitation they call me.

MOROS [*aside*].

    Arse-out-of-fashion, here is a mystication:

    Diricke Quintine will gather rods of the Pine-nut-tree,   505

    And beat mine arse till it be out of fashion.

    With this device truly I cannot agree.

DISCIPLINE.

    Why stand you murmuring there alone?

    Give ear unto the words that to you be said.

PIETY.

    Come Moros, come good son, I must be gone;   510

    To dwell with me you need not be afraid.

MOROS.

    Afraid? no, I will go with you to the world's end;

    I promise you to be true night and day,

    For though never so much about me you do spend,

    I will not bear the valor of a penny away.   515

                  Go before him and yet say.

---

498. Very ... Quintine] *Q*; Very ... maister *Brandl*.

515.1.] *Brandl notes the omission of two lines which would complete the rhyme scheme and clarify this S.D.*

---

498 ff.] All three of Moros' names depend upon similarities in sound; cf. ll. 311–314. The "quintine, quintain" was the post set up as a mark for tilting, and the word is used as a verb, meaning "to tilt at a target." In 1600 Will Kempe used the name "Derrick" as a verb: "One that would pol his father, derrick his Dad" (*OED*); he is, however, probably referring to the noted hangman at Tyburn whose surname was Derrick. *Out of fashion* (l. 506) means "out of shape."

504. *mystication*] seemingly a coined word, perhaps derived from medieval Latin "*mysticare*," meaning to explicate a secret sense (Du Cange, *Glossarium Mediae et Infimae Latinitatis* [Niort, 1885], V, 564).

515. *valor*] value.

PIETY.

We have taken a busy work upon us;
For all our words he is not the better one pease.

DISCIPLINE.

Well, a season with him take ye pain;
We will prove if we can do any good.

MOROS.

With them if long you do here remain,   520
I will go seek a new master by the rood.

Go out Piety *and* Moros.

EXERCITATION.

How think you? truly, I am in despair;
I fear that all our labor will be lost.
He is not bent neither to abstinence nor prayer;
I am advised to bestow on him no more cost.   525

DISCIPLINE.

Ipsaque non multo est natura potentior usu.
I like well that he is gone with Piety,
For conversation with persons of virtue
Altereth nature sometime for a surety;
Custom may all kind of manners bring forth.   530
This to be true we know by experience,
But if he decay we must take it at worth;
At the least let us do our diligence.

EXERCITATION.

If he had been taken somewhat in season,
I would have hoped in his amendment;   535

Between whiles let Moros *put in his head.*

But folly hath so overcharged his reason
That he is past redress in my judgment.
While a plant of a tree is young and tender,
You may cause it to grow crooked or right;
So a child, while knowledge is but slender,   540
You may instruct whereto you will by might.

521.1.] *Q prints in margin to the left of*   535.1.] *Q prints in margin to the left of*
ll. 521–522.   *ll. 535–537.*

517. *pease*] pea.
526. *Ipsaque . . . usu*] "The nature of a thing is not much improved by
use"; the Latin tag represents Discipline's agreement with Exercitation,
an agreement which is qualified in the succeeding lines.
529. *for a surety*] for certain.

But after the plant is grown to a tree,
To any bowing it will not give place;
So young folks, when to age grown they be,
Wax stubborn and be of an indurate face.   545
Again he is of a very haughty nature,
A wit, but to no goodness applied.
If he shall be suffered to endure,
Much evil by him shall be multiplied.

DISCIPLINE.

Let us see how he doth profit in piety.   550
If he goeth anything forward therein
Unto labor, virtue and verity,
I will hope him easily to win;
For as I said here a little before,
Whoso doth God faithfully serve and fear   555
And above all things him love and honor,
He shall thrive, go forward and prosper.

EXERCITATION.

I believe that with Piety he went
From correction himself to wind,
For if he to any virtue be bent,   560
I am much deceived truly in my mind.
Certain persons I could rehearse by name
Have pretended a great perfection,
And why? To avoid punishment and shame
Due for their vicious infection.   565
As some have enter'd into religion,
Wherefore? Because they will not pay their debt
When they are persons of no good devotion,
For upon vanity their hearts are set.

556. love] *this edn.*; serve *Q, Brandl*   566. have] *Brandl*; baue *Q*.
(*cf. ll. 207, 245*).

---

545. *indurate face*] hardened, obstinate appearance.

548. *endure*] to harden as well as to last; cf. "so endured with sin and vice is he" (*OED*).

559. *wind*] to turn from, escape.

566. *some . . . religion*] A. G. Dickens suggests that "religion" here refers to monastic life; one could not sue a "religious" for private debts because he lacked private property. The lines represent a survival of anti-monastic propaganda.

DISCIPLINE.

    Go we softly and hearken for his fashion.   570
    If with any lewdness I chance him to take,
    I shall minister to him such correction
    As shall make his flesh tremble and quake.

EXERCITATION.

    With Piety you are not like him to find,
    He did put in his head twice or thrice.   575
    He looketh for mates of another kind;
    Wholly he is given to folly and vice.

DISCIPLINE.

    He is like to escape very narrowly
    If neither of us catch him by the back;
    Except he be corrected thoroughly,   580
    He will still use his foolish knack.

                          Go out both.

        Here enter'th Idleness.

IDLENESS.

    Where the devil is the whoreson fool?
    He bad me even now come hither.
    Doubtless he is gone again to school,
    Even very now we were together.   585
    Truly, they will make him a fool indeed.
    Teach him good manners? Teach my dog!
    When you see him in learning proceed,
    Then will I make a man of this log.
    What ho! where art thou, Moros? what ho?   590
    Doubtless they take pain about a stone.
    Doting fools think to make corn to grow
    Upon gravel where earth there is none.

MOROS (*cry without the door, making a noise of beating*).

    Alas, alas, no more! no more, no more!

594.S.D. *cry . . . beating*] Q *prints in
margin to the left of ll. 594–597.*

  578–579.] i.e., if neither Exercitation nor Discipline are there to correct
Moros, he will only just escape damnation.
  589. *log*] perhaps the staff which Idleness carries.
  594.S.D. *cry . . . beating*] The stage direction indicates the limitations
of the company, for the actor speaks and produces the sound effects
simultaneously.

No more, good Master Diricke Quintine.   595
Body of God! you beat me so sore
I will forsake you and your doctrine.

IDLENESS.

No force hardily let them not spare.
What doth the fool in such company?
O, that they would beat him on the buttocks bare.   600
To see that I would spend an half penny.
What how, Moros? come hither I say.
He will not tarry long I dare warrant;
He and I meet ever once in a day.
Little will he stick to play the truant.   605

Here enter'th Incontinence.

INCONTINENCE.

What? Idleness, the parent of all vice,
Who thought to have found thee here?

IDLENESS.

Then art thou neither mannerly nor wise,
As by thy salutation doth appear;
For if I of vice be the parent,   610
Then thy parent I must needs be.
Thou art a vice by all men's consent;
Therefore, it is like that I begat thee.

INCONTINENCE.

My parent? then hang my parent!
No sir, I am your fellow and mate;   615
Therewith you may be well content,
For I am of no small estate:
Otium enim fomes vitiorum est otium mentem,
Ad multa mala trahit otii comes ipsa libido est—
Idleness of vices is a provocation,   620
To many evils Idleness draweth the mind.
Lust, or lecherous inclination,
Is fellow to Idleness by kind.

619. *trahit*] *Brandl*; Trahunt *Q*.

598. *hardily*] by all means.   605. *stick*] hesitate.
623. *by kind*] The relationship is established in terms of a similarity in
mode of operation: as Idleness draws the mind so Incontinence inclines
the mind.

Lo, I have proved by authority
That I am thy fellow, as I said;   625
To be my parent it were temerity.
Your argument here I have stayed.

IDLENESS.

They were thine own words and not mine.
The parent of all vice thou didst me call;
Then it followeth that I am thine,   630
For thou art the greatest vice of all.
The greatest mischief that ever chanced
Came by the means of inconstancy;
For whereas thou art enhanced,
There is all mischief and insolency.   635

Here enter'th Wrath.

WRATH.

Make room! stand back in the devil's name!
Stand back, or I will lay thee on the face.

INCONTINENCE.

Merry, stand thou back with a very shame.
Is there not room enough in the place?

IDLENESS.

It is but a copy of his countenance;   640
Wrath must declare his property.

INCONTINENCE.

He is as hot as a vengeance—
[*Aside.*]   Stand back and give him liberty.

---

624. *by authority*] "by quoting authority," i.e., the Latin tag.

626. *temerity*] rashness; cf. l. 655 "temerarious."

632. *greatest mischief*] The Fall in the Garden was in certain traditions the result of greed, gluttony and, in rabbinical traditions, lust.

633. *inconstancy*] incontinence; as a gloss of I Cor. 9:27, cf. "some do gather of this place, that Paul did mortify in himself the fire of inconstancy, by long fasting" (*OED*).

634. *enhanced*] exalted, elevated.

636.] Wrath cries out both to the characters on stage and to the audience; if the play was performed in a hall, there was probably no raised stage and the audience surrounded the actors on three sides.

640. *It*] i.e., his action.

WRATH.

    I had went it had been another,
    I thought to have given thee a blow;   645
    In my rage I favor not my brother.
    The nature of Wrath full well you do know.

IDLENESS.

    Wrath and madness they say be all one,
    Saving that madness doth still remain;
    But wrath in fools will soon be gone,   650
    Yea, and as soon it will come again.

INCONTINENCE.

    To fools not only incontinency
    Is annexed but wrath also furious;
    The mind of fools without clemency
    Soon waxeth hot and is temerarious.   655

WRATH.

    Speaking of fools, it cometh to my remembrance
    I thought to have found Moros, the fool, here.

IDLENESS.

    He goeth to school now with a vengeance,
    He shall be a doctor the next year.

WRATH.

    To school? ha, ha, ha, as angry as I am,   660
    I must laugh to hear of Moros such news.

IDLENESS.

    I spake with him as hither I came,
    And willed him their schooling to refuse.

INCONTINENCE.

    They keep him there still by violence,
    But I know that with us is his heart.   665

WRATH.

    When they bring Moros unto sapience,
    Then of my sword I will make a cart.

IDLENESS.

    I suppose that he will not be long hence
    If by any means he may escape.

INCONTINENCE.

    I dare wage with any man forty pence   670

---

644. *went*] thought.

To make him shortly as wise as an ape.

WRATH.

>That wager with thee durst I lay,
>To make him so wise, thou art not able;
>For he is as very a fool, I dare say,
>And as stark an idiot as ever bare bable.   675

IDLENESS.

>Yea, but he shall be a more fool yet
>When all we three be unto him annexed;
>For the truth is he hath now some wit,
>But then all his wits shall be perplexed.
>With me he is very well acquainted,   680
>For all his bringing up hath been with me,
>So that any virtue he could never see;
>Therefore, Pastime he calleth me alway.
>In plays and games he hath no measure.
>Incontinency, to him thou must say   685
>That thy name is called Pleasure.

INCONTINENCE.

>I am called so with them that be wise;
>Wrath is wont to be called Manhood.

WRATH.

>In good faith little needeth this device;
>To be called by our names is as good.   690
>Doth he know what Idleness doth mean?
>Knoweth he Incontinency to be lechery?
>He discerneth not clean from unclean;
>His mind is all set on foolery.

Here enter'th Moros *looking upon a book and oftentimes look behind him.*

IDLENESS.

>See, see! Would you judge him a fool   695
>So sadly as he readeth on his book?

682.] *Brandl suggests the omission of a line, but the rhyme scheme does not seem disordered.*

694.1.] *Q combines this S.D. with that at l. 702.1.*

---

675. *stark*] absolute.
675. *bable*] in the context the fool's bauble, the baton surmounted by a fantastically carved head with ass' ears.
696. *sadly*] resolutely.

INCONTINENCE.

Belike he cometh now from school;
On his lesson earnestly he doth look.

WRATH.

Have you seen a more foolish face?
I must laugh to see how he doth look.   700

IDLENESS.

Hold your peace a little space,
And hear him read upon his book.

[Moros] *read as fondly as you can devise. Laugh all three at his reading.*

MOROS.

Body of God! laugh you me to scorn?
I will tell Master Diricke Quintine—
By these ten bones I will, I have sworn—   705
And he shall teach you to make tile-pin.
Take heed of Arse-out-of-fashion;
I advise you, come not in his claws.
I will tell them by God's Passion
How you judge them fools and daws.   710
I would you were with Pine-nut-tree;
He would make you a little sadder.
You shall go up to the gallow tree
And come down without a ladder.

WRATH.

You are well-learned it doth appear,   715
Can you any Latin to us speak?

MOROS.

I can sing *Custodi nos* in the choir,
And a verse of course, finely broke.

INCONTINENCE.

Read you Latin or Greek in your book?
What was it, I pray you, let us know?   720

697. Belike] *this edn.*; By like *Q*,   702.1. *Laugh . . . reading*] *Q prints in
Brandl.*   *margin to the left of l. 694.1.*

702.1. *fondly*] foolishly.   705. *ten bones*] the ten fingers.
706. *tile-pin*] a peg of hardwood used to fasten tiles to the laths of a roof.
718. *verse*] perhaps the versicles in the liturgy or the sections of the
psalms or canticles which are sung responsively.
718. *broke*] cracked, due to the boy's changing voice.

MOROS.

Here, you may see if you will look.

It was the cuckold's crossrow.

IDLENESS.

That crossrow let us hear, I pray thee.

And a point for thy labor thou shalt have.

MOROS.

I am but a learner you may see;   725

I can no further than K for a knave.

God's santy, Pastime my playfellow,

For God's sake keep me from Diricke Quintine.

IDLENESS.

If my counsel thou wilt follow,

I will keep thee from him and from his doctrine.   730

INCONTINENCE.

He speaketh of one Diricke Quintine,

Pine-nut-tree and Arse-out-of-fashion;

Doth he not mean old Discipline,

Piety and Exercitation?

IDLENESS.

Yes pardy, but so to speak he cannot.   735

Tell him one thing twenty times,

And he will forget it by and by, God wot;

Yet can he sing songs and make rhymes.

WRATH.

What need we to change our names for him,

For he discerneth not cheese from chalk?   740

He careth not who doth sink or swim,

So that in his own ways he may walk.

MOROS.

Shall I speak with you, Pastime, in your ear?

A word or two I would tell you of my mind.

Mast. Pastime this same grim man I do fear,   745

Trow you that he will be my friend?

---

724. *point*] possibly a northern form of "pint."

735. *pardy*] by God; a mild oath which often meant no more than "verily."

737. *wot*] knows.

745. *Mast.*] abbreviated form of "master." Cf. l. 1307, note.

745. *grim*] fierce, cruel.

IDLENESS.

I warrant thee, all we be thy friends here;
We come to rid thee out of thy foe's bands.

INCONTINENCE.

Fear none of us, but be thou of good cheer.
Bid us welcome and take us by the hands.   750

MOROS (*take them by the hand*).

Bid us welcome and take us by the hands [*to* Idleness].
Bid us welcome and take us by the hands [*to* Incontinence].
Bid us welcome and take us by the hands [*to* Wrath].

WRATH.

Gramercy, Moros, how do you?

IDLENESS.

You are welcome Master Manhood, say.   755

MOROS.

You are welcome Master Robin-hood, say.

IDLENESS.

You shall cough me a fool, I make God a vow.

MOROS.

You shall cough me a fool, I make God a vow.

INCONTINENCE.

I can laugh well at him by this day.

MOROS.

I can laugh well at him by this day.   760

IDLENESS.

Come to me, Moros. What dost thou with this book?
Thou canst not read upon it, I am sure.

MOROS.

Pine-nut-tree took it me thereon to look;
There are goodly saints in it, fair and pure.

WRATH.

Alas, one word to read in it he is not able;   765
More fools than he to give him a book.
A fool will delight more in a bable,
And more meet for him thereon to look.

751.S.D. *take . . . hand*] *Q prints in*   768. thereon] *Brandl*; thereou *Q*.
margin to the left of ll. 752–753.

757. *cough me a fool*] make a fool of me.
763. *took*] gave.

IDLENESS.

Look what a book I have for thee here.

Have a pair of cards ready.

Cast away that book; it is worse than nought.   770

INCONTINENCE.

This book will make thee of a lusty cheer
If thou wilt bear it alway in thy thought.

MOROS.

God's days, it is a goodly book indeed.
Santy amen! here are saints a great sort.
This book passeth "Christ's cross me speed."   775
Ha, ha, ha, to he, ha, ha, ha! here is goodly sport.
But let not Diricke Quintine this book see;
He did set me a lesson to can.

WRATH.

None of them all shall meddle with thee;
We are come to make thee a man.   780

IDLENESS.

Make curtsy and say, "I thank you, Manhood."

MOROS.

Make curtsy and say, "I thank you, Robin-hood."

Make curtsy backward.

Gods, see here is a goodly gentlewoman,
Here are specks—some black, some red as blood.
Teach me this book, I pray you, perfectly to can.   785

IDLENESS.

If I wist that thou wouldst be pretty and wise,
I would give thee other things therewith to play.
Seest thou these bones? These are a pair of dice.
I will teach thee to occupy them one day.

MOROS.

You taught me first to play at blow point,   790

769.1. *pair*] Q (*which prints S.D. in*   782.1.] Q *prints in margin to the left of*
margin to the left of ll. 770–772); pack   *ll. 782–783.*
Brandl.

769.1. *pair*] set, pack.   778. *can*] learn, study.
786. *wist*] knew.   786. *pretty*] clever, artful.   789. *occupy*] use.
790. *blow point*] probably blowing an arrow through a tube at numbers,
perhaps a lottery game.

At span-counter, quoiting, and mosell-the-peg,
At skayles, and the playing with a sheep's joint,
And to hop a good way on my one leg.
How long was I learning of these plays?
I am apt enough such good things to take.   795
Do you no more but show me the ways
And, if I learn not, let me lose the stake.

IDLENESS.

Look what I have done for thee beside.
Here have I gotten thee company,
Whithersoever thou wilt go or ride,   800
To defend thee from all villainy.
Lo this gentleman is called Pleasure.
He will teach thee to handle a wench;
Means I will teach thee to get treasure,
For such things we will make a trench.   805

MOROS.

Sir, is your name called Play-sure?
You are welcome, I thank you heartily.

INCONTINENCE.

Tush fool, my name is called Pleasure,
That is liking and lust bodily.
Fools love alway such dalliance,   810
To kiss, to clip, and in bed to play.
O, with lusty girls to sing and dance,
To have a more pleasant life no man may.

MOROS.

O I mean what you know now.
Master Pastime, hark again in your ear.   815

IDLENESS.

Tush, tush, I warrant thee, care not thou.
I will provide for all such gear.
Lo, this is Manhood to make thee bold;

---

791. *span-counter*] a game in which one player seeks to throw his counters
so close to those of his opponent that the distance between them could be
spanned by a hand.
792. *skayles*] skittles.
792. *sheep's joint*] knucklebones or jackstones.
800. *go*] walk.   805. *trench*] device.

Let there be but a word and a blow.

MOROS.

I would look big like a man; that I would 820
If my beard would a little more grow.

WRATH.

Suffer no man with thee to reason,
For fools can no wise answer make;
Therefore, give a blow alway in season,
Pass not thou how they do it take; 825
Like a man ever face out the matter,
Stick not blood, heart, and wounds to swear;
But suffer no man with thee to clatter,
Anon let him have a blow on the ear.
Behold, here I give thee a good sword 830
And a dagger thyself to defend;
Draw thy dagger at every word,
And say that thy blood thou wilt spend.

MOROS.

Bold, quoth he! I pray you keep my book,
These weapons have set me on a fire. 835

Flourish with your sword.

How say you? like a man do I not look?
To be fighting now is all my desire;
No remedy, with one of you I must fight.
Fend your heads, you fools, knaves, and daws.

IDLENESS.

He showeth the nature of a fool right, 840
Which is to chide and fight without a cause.

INCONTINENCE.

It is a proverb wise and ancient:
Beware how you give any edge-tool
Unto madmen that be insipient,
Unto a young child, and unto a fool. 845

835.1.] *Q prints in margin to the left of*
ll. 836–837.

825. *Pass not*] care not.   828. *clatter*] chatter, talk idly.
843. *edge-tool*] any implement with a cutting edge; for the proverbial
expression "to jest with edge-tools," cf. *Enough*, l. 518.
844. *insipient*] foolish.

-37-

WRATH.

> He fighteth till he is out of breath.
> Enough now, Moros, it is well done.

MOROS.

> By the mass, I will fight myself to death;
> I pray you, let not me leave so soon.

INCONTINENCE.

> Sirrah, who am I? Will you remember?   850
> What did Pastime tell you in your ear?

MOROS.

> A pretty morsel, young and tender—
> Now would to God I were there.

IDLENESS.

> Thou must wear thy sword by thy side,
> And thy dagger handsomely at thy back;   855
> Before thou fightest thou must use to chide.
> Mark what I say and learn of me that knack.
> First, this order with thee we will take:
> We will teach thee to play at cards and dice,
> Acquainted with Nell and Nan we will thee make,   860
> And to appear a man both mighty and wise.
> We will desire Pleasure to take pain
> To provide us an handsome hospital
> Where secretly we may together remain
> Till we have finished our devices all.   865

INCONTINENCE.

> Hark, is it best that there we meet
> At that house such as we use to banquet?

MOROS.

> Nay, I pray you, let us have one sheet,
> For I cannot well lie in a blanket.

IDLENESS.

> Tush fool, we speak of banqueting;   870
> We mean to eat, drink, and make good cheer,
> With Meg and Bess to be ruffling

---

863. *hospital*] place of lodging but also a house of entertainment; in pre-Reformation days hospitals were part of the Church's charitable program and therefore objects of Reformation satire.

872. *ruffling*] swaggering.

Whereas no pleasure shall be too dear.

WRATH.

There are beds, blankets, and sheets good store,
And the house of a girl never empty; 875
You shall be sure of one or other evermore.
Sometime you may have your choice of twenty.

INCONTINENCE.

You mean the thacked house by the waterside
Which is whitelimed above in the loof?

IDLENESS.

Yea, pardy, there thou shalt for us provide; 880
An house it is for the nonce, if it come to the proof.

INCONTINENCE.

I go hence. Tarry you not after long,
For I will bid mine hostess make haste.

MOROS.

Before you go, let us have a song;
I can retch up to sing sol, fa, and past. 885

IDLENESS.

Thou hast songs good store, sing one,
And we three the foot will bear.

MOROS.

Let me study, it will come anon.
Pepe la, la, la—it is too high there;
So ho, ho—and that is too low; 890
Soll, soll, fa, fa—and that is too flat;
Re, re, re—by and by you shall know;
Mi, mi, mi—how say you to that?

IDLENESS.

Care not for the true, but what is thy song;
No remedy, thou must first begin. 895

INCONTINENCE.

I will be gone if you tarry long,
When we know how, we shall come in.

894. true] Q; tune *Brandl.*

---

878. *thacked*] thatched.
879. *loof*] loft.
881. *proof*] test in law court.
885. *retch*] stretch, reach.   894. *true*] true pitch.

MOROS.	I have a pretty titmouse
	Come picking on my toe,
ALL FOUR.	Gossip, with you I purpose 900
	To drink before I go.

MOROS.	Little pretty nightingale
	Among the branches green,
ALL FOUR.	Give us of your Christmas ale
	In the honor of Saint Stephen. 905

MOROS.	Robin Redbreast with his notes,
	Singing aloft in the choir,
ALL FOUR.	Warneth to get you frieze coats
	For winter then draweth near.

MOROS.	My bridle lieth on the shelf; 910
	If you will have any more,

Go out Incontinence.

Vouchsafe to sing it yourself,
For here you have all my store.

WRATH.

A song much like th'author of the same;
It hangeth together like feathers in the wind.   915

MOROS.

This song learned I of my dame,
When she taught me mustard seed to grind.
God's days, is Play-sure gone away?
I would have spoken with him or ever he had gone.
I am sorry for that, by this day;   920
He should have borne me a token to Joan.

IDLENESS.

Thou shalt bear four quarters of a fool.

900, 904, 908.S.P. ALL FOUR.] *this edn.*; All iiii. the same. *Q*, *Brandl.*
910. bridle] *this edn.*; brigle *Q*, *Brandl* (*cf. l. 100*).

911.1.] *Q prints in margin to the left of ll. 911–912.*
914. th'author] *this edn.*; thauthour *Q*, *Brandl.*

898–913.] Brandl treats the stanzas as separate songs, but the stanzas seem related.
907, 909. *choir . . . near*] The Quarto spellings, *quere*, *nere* suggest the rhyme.
908. *frieze*] coarse woolen cloth.
915. *feathers . . . wind*] Tilley, F 163; cf. *Enough*, l. 158.

Perdy, Joan will that best regard.

MOROS.

    Shall we go leap over the stool,

    Or play for the hole about the churchyard?   925

    I must be doing of somewhat alway.

    My weapon once again I must handle.

    How my dagger will cut now I will assay.

    Beware how with me they wandle.

    Fend your heads. How like you this flourish?   930

    Nay, I can fetch him over my head.

    This fetch among such as be foolish,

    I may tell you, will stand sometime in stead.

WRATH.

    This fellow fighteth very sore alone.

    God have mercy on his soul he will kill.   935

    This fury will away anon,

    Namely when he is acquainted with Jill.

IDLENESS.

    Keep thy fighting till Discipline doth come;

    Then let me see how thou wilt play the man.

MOROS.

    Body of God, stand away. Make room.   940

    I will surely hit him if I can.

    O that my sword were a mile long,

    I would kill him then whereas he dwelleth.

    Methink I am waxen very strong;

    See, I pray you, how my heart swelleth.   945

Here enter'th Discipline.

DISCIPLINE.

    The longer thou livest, the more fool thou art.

933. stead] *this edn.*; steads *Q*;
steade *Brandl.*

---

  924. *leap . . . stool*] a version of leap frog.

  925. *play . . . hole*] If not a marble game, this is probably the old game in which balls were rolled through arches.

  929. *wandle*] *OED* gives "to walk unsteadily" but context here suggests "meddle"; cf. l. 1344.

  932. *fetch*] sweeping movement of the sword, but also trick, stratagem.

  935.] elliptic construction; i.e., "on his soul [whom] he will kill."

A fool in childhood, a fool in adolency,
In man's state thou wilt play a fool's part.

Let Moros *let fall his sword and hide him.*

And as a fool die with shame and infamy.
Beat a fool in a mortar, saith the wise man, 950
And thou shalt not make him leave his folly.
I have done all that ever I can,
And I see it profiteth not, truly.

MOROS.

Save me, I pray you, Master Robin-hood.
This is Diricke Quintine my master. 955
He will fight as he were wood;
For me he hath brought yonder waster.
I know Diricke Quintine's intent.
He will bring me to Arse-out-of-fashion;
There in work and labor I shall be pent, 960
And I had lever die, by God's passion.

WRATH.

Why whoreson, take thy sword in thy hand,
And at the gainest upon him lay.

IDLENESS.

Go to him like a man, by thee I will stand;
Not so—hardy in his head one word say. 965

MOROS.

Sirrah, speak you, I pray you, Robin-hood,
Take you my sword and drive him hence.

WRATH.

What, whoreson, I tell thee my name is Manhood.
I had lever have spent forty pence.

DISCIPLINE.

Animi vilis timor argumentum est; 970
Fear of a vile mind is an argument.

947. adolency] *Brandl*; vdolencie   948.1.] *Q prints in margin to the left*
Q.   *of ll. 948–951.*

---

947. *adolency*] adolescence.
950–951. *Beat . . . folly*] Prov. 27:22.
956. *wood*] mad.   957. *waster*] cudgel, staff.
963. *at the gainest*] by the shortest way.
969. *forty pence*] customary amount for a wager.
971.] i.e., "fear is an argument (proof) of a vile mind."

Conscience accuseth the foolish beast
That he hath forsaken wholesome document.
MOROS.

    I shall have a beard, I trow, one day.
    Then shall I be a man strong and bold;   975
    If my beard were grown, to you I may say
    I would pay him home, by God, that I would.
WRATH.

    Take thy sword in thine hand and say,
    "I defy thee, aye old rusty peasant."
MOROS.

    Take thy sword in thine hand and say,   980
    "I defy thee, aye old thirsty weasant."
WRATH.

    Avoid, trudge, and get thee away,
    Or by his heart I will cut thy weasant.
MOROS.

    Accloyed grudge but not denay,
    Or by his cart I will pluck a pheasant.   985
IDLENESS.

    Why, it is true that of thee he said,
    "The longer thou livest, the more fool thou art."
MOROS.

    Body of God, of him I am so afraid
    That at every word I am like to fart.
WRATH.

    The fool as yet is young and nesh,   990
    And the fear of Discipline is in his mind;
    After that he is nuzzled in woman's flesh,
    The knave he will play in his kind.

984. Accloyed] *this edn.*; A cloyde
Q, *Brandl.*

---

973. *document*] teaching, instruction.
979. *rusty*] churlish, foul.
981. *weasant*] weasand, windpipe.
984–985.] Moros mis-repeats Wrath's dismissal and reduces it to nonsense; *accloyed* means "surfeited" while *grudge*, probably coined to parallel "trudge," means "one who murmurs." *Denay* is an archaic Middle English form of "deny."
990. *nesh*] timid.

IDLENESS.

It is even so; a boy is never bold
Till he hath companied with an whore,   995
Then doth he pick quarrels, chide and scold;
After that he despiseth both rich and poor.
Come, Pleasure hath all things provided;
Let us no longer tarry here.
He will think that we have him derided;   1000
Go we, let us see his provision and cheer.

MOROS.

I will be sure to be gone first.
I am out of your hands, Diricke Quintine;
Now do thou thy best and thy worst,
I defy both thee and all thy doctrine.   1005

Go out all three.

DISCIPLINE.

Mark the trade of much youth at this day,
See if this fool painteth not out their image;
Them they despise that either do or say
Anything at all to restrain their dotage.
The fool and boy, saith the prophet Esaye,   1010
Shall presume against his ruler ancient.
Young fools do this saying verify.
To wise men it is over-evident,
When fools are suffer'd in folly
And youth maintained in their will,   1015
When they come up to man's state wholly,
Fools they be and so they continue still.
One writeth thus among many things,
Never shall you have good men and sapient
Where there be no good children and younglings,   1020
Which thing is most true in my judgment.
Two things destroy youth at this day:
Indulgentia parentum, the fondness of parents
Which will not correct their naughty way,

1006. *trade*] manner, way of life.
1009. *dotage*] stupidity, folly, applied here to youth, not age.
1010. *Esaye*] Isaiah; the allusion may however be to Prov. 15:5.
1023. *Indulgentia parentum*] the indulgence of parents.

But rather embolden them in their intents; 1025
Idleness, alas idleness, is another.
Whoso passeth through England,
To see the youth he would wonder,
How idle they be and how they stand;
A Christian man's heart it would pity 1030
To behold the evil bringing up of youth.
God preserve London, that noble city,
Where they have taken a godly order, for a truth;
God give them the minds the same to maintain,
For in the world is not a better order. 1035
If it may be God's favor still to remain,
Many good men will be in that border. *Go out.*

[*Enter* Fortune.]

FORTUNE.

No God's mercy? no reverence? no honor?
No cap off? no knee bowed? no homage?
Who am I? is there no more good manner? 1040
I trow, you know not me nor my lineage.
I tell you, I rule and govern all;
I advance and I pluck down again;
Of him that of birth is poor and small,
As a noble man I can make to reign; 1045
I am she that may do all things.
In heaven or earth who is like to me?
I make captives of lords and kings,
Of captives or fools I make kings to be.
No curtsey yet for all this power? 1050
I tell you learned men call me a goddess.

1050. for] *Brandl*; sor *Q*.

1030. *it would pity*] impersonal construction.
1032–1033.] London's laws for apprenticeship and for handling vagabonds were influential in framing the Statute of Artificers in 1563; cf. W.
Cunningham, *The Growth of English Industry and Commerce* (Cambridge,
1925), pp. 27–37.
1037. *in that border*] within that city.
1037.1. *Fortune*] As Craik suggests (p. 63), Fortune probably carries her
symbolic wheel; it is doubtful, however, that she is blindfolded, since she
comments that the audience has not paid her proper homage.

A beggar I make rich in an hour;
To such as I love, I give good success.
Who in this world can me withstand?
Who can say yea, where I say nay?   1055
I change all in the turning of a hand;
Whatsoever I will, do it I may.
Have I done nothing for any here?
Have I not one lover nor friend?
None to welcome me with a merry cheer?   1060
Now by my truth you be unkind.
Well, I may chance some to displease,
I purpose to dally and play a feat
Which shall turn some to small ease;
A popish fool will I place in a wiseman's seat.   1065
By that you shall learn, I trow,
To do your duty to a lady so high;
He shall teach you Fortune to know
And to honor her till you die.

[*Enter* Incontinence.]

INCONTINENCE.

It is a world to see the fool's greediness.   1070
I have nuzzled him in carnality;
A man would marvel to see his readiness
Unto all fleshly sensuality.
And these harlots are not to learn
How to dally with a simple fool.   1075
They may lead him with a thread of yarn
Into the midst of a whirlpool.
He prayed me hither to decline
And look diligently about.
He is afraid of Discipline   1080
And of Exercitation no doubt;
Neither of them both can I see.
I will return and bear him word,

1071. in carnality] *Brandl*; incar-
nalitie *Q*.

_____

1070. *It . . . world*] "it's a marvel."
1078. *decline*] turn aside.

A glad man then will Moros be,
For them he feareth more than the sword.   1085

Semble a going out.

FORTUNE.

Whither now, sirrah? Are you blind?
Am I so little a mote that you cannot see?
I will pluck down your high mind
And cause you, I trow, to know me.

INCONTINENCE.

I cry you mercy, lady most excellent;   1090
Without doubt I did not your honor behold,
O Empress, O Goddess omnipotent,
I render you praises manifold.

FORTUNE.

Well, at this time I hold you excused,
Glad to see you do your duty so well.   1095
If all other had themselves so used,
It had been better for them, to you I may tell.
I trow your name is Incontinency,
One of the properties of Moros.

INCONTINENCE.

I see him given to insolency,   1100
And I further him in that purpose.
Lechery is to fools connatural;
Wisemen thereof are ever ware,
For they see that such uses bestial
Bring men to infamy, shame and care.   1105

FORTUNE.

How vile soever he be in condition,
How foolish soever and insipient,
How full of pride soever and ambition,
How lecherous soever and incontinent,
It is not withstanding our pleasure   1110
To exalt him in honor and richesse.

1085.1.] *Q prints in margin to the right*   1102. connatural] *Brandl*; couna-
of ll. 1085–1086.   tural *Q.*

1099. *properties*] attributes.
1102. *connatural*] a native characteristic.
1111. *richesse*] wealth.

We will give him laud, wealth and treasure
And in all things therewith good success.
He loveth women, I will give him plenty;
He loveth gay raiment, meats and drinks fine,   1115
Of raiment he shall have shifts twenty,
Store of venison, wildfowl, bread and wine.
Moros shall lack nothing for a season.
They shall see that Fortune can exalt fools
Who shall nurture men of wit and reason   1120
And make them glad to learn their schools.
Seeing that the vulgars will me not praise
For exalting good men and sapient,
I will get me a name another ways,
That is, by erecting fools insipient.   1125

INCONTINENCE.

Pleaseth it you to give me license
A few verses of a poet to recite?

FORTUNE.

I will gladly hear the poet's sentence
Whereas against me he doth not write.

INCONTINENCE.

Sed redeo ad stultos, quos quando extollit et alto,   1130
Collocat in soleo, cupiens fortuna iocari,
O quod stultitiis tunc omnia plena videbis.
I come now to speak of fools again
With whom, when it pleaseth Fortune to play,
She extolleth and maketh to reign,   1135
Yea, and to them wise men to obey.
O then with how many follies shalt thou see
All things filled and replenished,
Which to rehearse long it would be,
Yet of the poet they be published.   1140
Dishonesty mightily triumpheth then;
Virtusque mouet contempta cachinnum
(Virtue is mocked of every man);
Then of whores and harlots there is no small sum.
Nothing but eating, drinking, and play,   1145

1112. laud] *Q*; lande *Brandl.*   1136. Yea] *this edn.*; Ye *Q, Brandl.*

1121. *schools*] doctrine.

−48−

Only voluptuousness foolish and filthy,
Increaseth more and more day by day
And hath the rule in realm and city.

FORTUNE.

And as the poet writeth so shall it be;
With Moros we will take such an order   1150
That all things which for his pleasure he shall see
So let him command in every border.
You know where Moros we shall find;
We command you to lead us to the place,
And forasmuch as you occupy his mind,   1155
So teach him to know our noble grace;
For before that he doth again appear,
Another manner of person we will him make;
Yea, and we will cause all persons far and near
As a worthy gentleman him to take.   1160

INCONTINENCE.

If it will please your grace to walk,
I will bring you whereas Moros is.

FORTUNE.

Come, wait upon me; by the way we will talk.
Thou shalt see wonders after this.   *Go out both.*

[*Enter* Piety.]

PIETY.

I am come hither now to complain   1165
Not only to see this fool thus to miscarry,
Which virtuous Discipline both disdain
And to honesty is contrary,
But also of a great multitude
Which despise God and his counsel,   1170
As though there were no beatitude,
No torments for sin with devils in hell.
I can say no more of Piety
Than I have said a little before,
Which is to serve God's majesty,   1175
The same to love, to fear, to honor.
But now, alas, what manners, what heavy times,

1165. *complain*] lament.

Piety is utterly extinguished.
What contempt is there, what crimes,
More mischief than can be published;   1180
And as God's majesty is despised,
So the love among men doth abate.
Never was there greater hatred devised
Than is among men of every estate;
What falsehood, what deceit, and guile?   1185
What subtilties are of men invented?
Who doth not his body with sin defile?
Who is with his own state contented?
I have read of many worlds and seasons;
Of so sinful a world did I never read.   1190
About mischief men occupy their reasons,
None other thing nowadays is in their head;
Yet God hath some good people, I dare say,
Which pray devoutly, fast and abstain
And call upon him night and day   1195
The wickedness of our times to restrain.
And I doubt not for his own name sake,
He will subvert the works of sin
Which he grant shortly to slake,
And that virtue the victory may win.   1200

[*Enter* Wrath.]

WRATH.

Ha, ha, ha! I must laugh to see Fortune's dalliance.
Lord, how she hath this fool enhanced.
The sport is to see his countenance;
This wealth hath to him strangely chanced.
But they say that fools are fortunable;   1205
It appeareth to be the true now indeed.
Fortune hath made a fool honorable,
And like more in honor to proceed;
Now am I sent officers to seek,
Impiety, Cruelty, and Ignorance.   1210
I must trudge about all this week,

1180. *mischief*] misfortune, evil.
1199. *slake*] diminish.

Not a little unto my hindrance.

PIETY.

    Such a master, such servants indeed!
    O what a plague is it evermore
    When virtuous men have evil speed,   1215
    And fools have ease, wealth and honor!
    Have we not had manifest probation?
    Have not men of God been put to silence?
    And such fools in whom was no good disputation,
    But altogether with cruelty gave they sentence?   1220

WRATH.

    Thou art one of them for whom I seek,
    Not for thy honor but for thy decay.
    I have commandment to chop thee as a leek
    If thou wilt not get thee away.
    Wherefore be ruled by my counsel,   1225
    Come no more into Moros' company,
    For both with shame he will expel
    And put thee also to villainy.

PIETY.

    Better it is to meet a she-bear
    When she is robbed of her whelps   1230
    Than with a fool that rule doth bear,
    For nother reason nor learning will be his helps.

WRATH.

    No moe words, but get thee away at once.
    I am Wrath, soon kindled and set on fire.
    Speak one word and I will break thy bones,   1235
    And tread thee down here in the mire.   [*Go out* Piety.]
    Yea, I advise thee, lo what Wrath can do.
    To Wrath place to give he is glad;
    To fools many are glad to lean to
    For fear of their rage when they are mad.   1240

1240. mad] *this edn.*; made *Q*,
Brandl.

1218–1220.] The obvious reference is to the Marian persecutions and to
the trials of Latimer and Cranmer; it is possible, however, that the lines
echo the current controversy over vestments.
    1228. *put . . . to villainy*] insult, injure.   1232. *nother*] neither.
    1239. *lean to*] defer to.

Yonder cometh one that I seek for;
I am deceived if it be not the same.
As he were blind, about he doth pore,
Ignorance I suppose is his name.

[*Enter* Ignorance.]

IGNORANCE.

Is there anybody here in this place?   1245
I am sent for in all the haste I ween;
I am commanded to come away apace.
They will marvel where so long I have been.

WRATH.

Whither should you go, I pray you, friend?
And who is it that for you did send?   1250

IGNORANCE.

Lady Fortune did tell me her mind,
And to speak with Moros I do intend.

WRATH.

To tarry here if you will take the pain,
Moros will come hither anon.
Where Impiety is I would know fain,   1255
And where I should speak with him alone.

IGNORANCE.

Crudelity, Impiety and I
Were coming all three together.
I think verily that they are passed by
And gone even the right way thither.   1260

WRATH.

What are their names when they come there?
What do you call Impiety?

IGNORANCE.

Philosophy his name is everywhere,
Crudelity Prudence, and I Antiquity.

WRATH.

Very well I am glad of this indeed,   1265
By reason hereof my journey is at an end.
I purpose no further to proceed;

1263. is] *Brandl*; his *Q*.

1257. *Crudelity*] variant form of "cruelty."

−52−

To return again I do intend.
I will cause Moros to make haste;
Antiquity tarrieth for you, I will say.   1270

IGNORANCE.

Yea, and though the time be somewhat past,
Tell him that I did not well know the way.

Go out Wrath.

Ignorance, yea Ignorance is my name,
A meet mate with fools to dwell,
A quality of an ancient fame;   1275
And yet drown I many one in hell.
The papists which the truth do know,
Lord, how I have nuzzled them in my science;
I have so taught them that howsoever the wind blow,
They shall still incline to my sentence,   1280
So that though they have knowledge and cunning,
They are but ignorant and fools.
After every heresy and popery they are running,
And delight daily to learn at new schools.
Also many that do themselves abuse,   1285
Some in that iniquity and some in this,
By ignorance they do themselves excuse,
As though they know not that they did amiss
When their conscience bear them record
That their acts are wicked and evil;   1290
Therefore, when they shall come before the Lord,
He shall condemn them with Satan the devil.

Moros *enter gaily disguised and with a foolish beard* [*with him* Cruelty *and* Impiety].

MOROS.

Ah sir, my beard is well grown.
I thought that I should be a man once,
Yea, a gentleman, and so will I be known,   1295
A man of honor both body and bones.
How say you, my counselors, tell me,
Have I not a gentleman's countenance?

1272.1.] *Q prints in margin to the*   1292.1–2.] *Q prints in margin to the*
right of ll. 1271–1272.   *left of ll. 1294–1298.*

IMPIETY.

A better face truly I did never see,
Nor a better leg in my remembrance. 1300

CRUELTY.

If you had not been comely and wise,
Fortune would not have so favored you.
You must appear to be strange and nice;
That will cause men humbly to bow.

IGNORANCE.

God's dainty, is this Master Moros? 1305
A proper gentleman, by Saint Ann!
To dwell with your Maship I purpose
And to do you the best service that I can.

IMPIETY.

This is another of your counsel,
Whose name is called Antiquity. 1310
His words are truer than the Gospel,
A person full of truth and fidelity.

MOROS.

You are welcome, gentle Sanguinity.
Ah sir? Is Sanguinity your name?

CRUELTY.

He is called ancient Antiquity, 1315
A person of good stock and great fame.

MOROS.

Welcome again then, gentle Tandidity

1303. *nice*] fastidious, precise.
1305. *God's dainty*] God's dignity, honor; the expression preserves the meaning of the French and Latin roots.
1307. *Maship*] abbreviated form of "mastership," which often implied disrespect.
1311–1312.] Antiquity represents the Catholic argument of the supremacy of tradition over Scripture (cf. ll. 1277 ff.).
1313. *Sanguinity*] If Moros is indulging in malapropism, his error is wittily to the point, for the word derives from the medieval Latin "*sanquinitas*" (blood-relationship), and Ignorance and the fool Moros are indeed closely related.
1317.] *Tandidity*] derived from "tantity," meaning "the fact of being or having so much" which describes antiquity.

And you are welcome, all three indeed—
Pild-lousy Boy, Fip-pence and Tandidity.
How do you, welcome all, good speed.   1320

IMPIETY.

Forsooth, I am called Philosophy.
Prudence is this man's name, doubtless.
Antiquity he is called, verily,
As hereafter we shall more plainly express.

MOROS.

Pild-lousy Boy, Fip-pence, and Tandidity,   1325
You are welcome. You come to wait on me?

IGNORANCE.

Yea, and to serve you with all humility
And to fulfill your requests ready to be.

IMPIETY.

Fortune appointed me to be governor,
Of your own person you to direct,   1330
And to convince every vain troubler
Which shall presume your mind to infect.

CRUELTY.

And me she appointed them to correct
Which should do ought against your mind,
Yea, and your profits and rents to collect   1335
And to seek narrowly where we may them find.

IGNORANCE.

I am ordained alway to give you warning
Of exercitation in any science,
Less you hurt your wits with learning,
And dull your understanding and science.   1340

MOROS.

Shall I tell you there was one Pine-nut-tree

1318. indeed—] in deede. *Brandl*;
indeeee. *Q*.

1319. *Pild-lousy*] *pild* means naked, bald.
1319. *Fip-pence*] five pence.
1331. *convince*] overcome.   1336. *narrowly*] carefully, closely.
1337. *ordained*] appointed, but also with theological overtones for
Ignorance is dressed as a priest.
1339. *Less*] lest.

Who a while had me in his handling;
He was up with God and holy divinity,
But I was soon weary of his wandling.
And that cursed whoreson Diricke Quintine   1345
Would beat me shrewdly, by God's passion;
He went about me to famish and pine
Through one Arse-out-of-fashion.
I shall desire you, Pild-lousy Boy,
And you, Fip-pence and Tandidity,   1350
Them to banish and utterly destroy,
For I fear their crudelity.

IMPIETY.

Fear? and you a man of nobility?
Remember that you are come to manhood.

CRUELTY.

Hath not Fortune set you in authority?   1355
With your own hand let their heart blood.

MOROS.

Body of God! give me my sword.
Heart, wounds! I will kill them by and by.
Arms and sides! I have spoken the word.
His blood and bones! they shall die.   1360
Am I in authority do you say?
May I hang, burn, head and kill?
Let them be sure I will do what I may;
I will be known in authority, that I will.

IMPIETY.

Piety, Discipline, and Exercitation—   1365
Mean you not them, I pray you?

MOROS.

They indeed have put me to tribulation,
But I trow I will trouble them again now.
Body of God! am I in authority?
I will burn them, hang them, and boil them.   1370

1343. divinity] *this edn.*; diuintre   1344. soon] sone *Q*; sore *Brandl.*
Q, Brandl.

1343. *divinity*] The Quarto spelling (*diuintre*) indicates the rhyme with
l. 1341.
1356. *let*] shed.

As many as once profess piety,
If I may know it, I will turmoil them.
IMPIETY.
Of God indeed many of them talk,
And of the soul, and of heaven and hell;
But from you as fools let them walk,   1375
They speak of a thing whereof they cannot tell.
I am named Philosophy,
The knowledge of all things I do contain.
In me is astronomy and astrology;
The truth of all things in me do remain.   1380
I can teach you heaven to know,
Which they call a spherical figure
More perfect than any other high or low,
Eternal forsooth in his own nature;
Also how that the world was made;   1385
In the midst of the said heaven,
How five suns divide it in their trade;
Of the cycles and epicycles seven;
Of moving and quiet I can teach;
Of matter and form I can tell goodly gear.   1390
Such as go up into pulpits and preach,
Especially these new fellows, to them give no ear;
Nay then, whereas you have authority,
Suffer them not in any wise to dwell.
Be bold to punish them with austerity,   1395

1386. In] *Brandl*; Iu *Q*.

1372. *turmoil*] disturb, harass.

1377. *Philosophy*] The satire here is directed against scholasticism.

1387. *five suns*] the five planets: Saturn, Jupiter, Mars, Venus, Mercury; they divide the *heaven* because they are, as the name "planet" suggests, the wandering stars.

1387. *trade*] path.

1388. *epicycles*] The theory of epicycles in Ptolemaic astronomy accounted for the "retrograde" motion of the planets when as a result of the combined motions of the earth and the planets about the sun the planets appeared to travel backward in a great loop.

1389. *moving and quiet*] The problem involves whether the earth was stationary or moving; the discussion of the problem is central to Copernicus' arguments in *De Revolutionibus*.

1390. *gear*] discourse, doctrine in a depreciatory sense.

For it is but all heresy that they do tell.
Goodly doctrines I can teach you of nature,
And how it bringeth forth nothing perfectly
Without art; this is a doctrine sure;
Also how the same worketh secretly.   1400
Now such as of God to you will talk
Of heaven, hell, or of the soul,
From your presence bid them walk,
Yea, though they allege Christ and Paul;
Concerning those things I am appointed   1405
To bring you into the verity.
Endeavor yourself to be acquainted
With your noble counselor Antiquity;
From time to time evermore still
He shall in your company remain.   1410
Prudence shall get in, poll and pill,
Forevermore seek for your gain.

MOROS.

You are a cunning person, I see that;
Would to God you had a better name—
Pild-lousy Boy, fie, that is too flat.   1415
And to call you Fip-pence, it is a shame.

IGNORANCE.

His name, I tell you, is Philosophy,
In whom is contained all science;
Antiquity is my name, verily,
And this person is called Prudence.   1420

MOROS.

God's blessing on your hearts all;
I shall remember your names, I trow.
My servants by their names I will call
If my beard a little longer would grow.

IMPIETY.

I doubt not but as you grow in age,   1425
So you will increase in sapience;

1407. yourself] *Brandl*; your felfe   1425. S.P. IMPIETY] *Brandl*; *not in Q.*
Q.

1411. *poll and pill*] to strip bare, plunder.

You shall never want a witty page
To sharpen your intelligence.

IGNORANCE.

With all your affairs let us alone,
Give you your mind to pleasure,   1430
Eat, drink, dally and play with Joan;
We will maintain your state with treasure.
Some will move you to read Scripture;
Some would have you seen in stories;
Some to feats of arms will you allure;   1435
All these are but plain vain glories.
Marry, I would have you seen in cards and dice,
As you shall be, I trow, within a while.
We trust to make you in them so wise
That none shall be able you to beguile.   1440

CRUELTY.

You must set yourself forth with the best;
You must learn to have a diverse countenance,
Frowning when a thing you shall detest,
Pleasant when ought is for your furtherance.
So, lo, that is well when you are angry,   1445
Meetly well too when you are pleased.
A smiling countenance you must carry
When your conceit is in all things eased.

IMPIETY.

By my troth, wot you like whom he doth look?
He is as like a cousin of mine as ever I did see. 1450

CRUELTY.

That he is like him in face you may swear on a book,
And also his conditions with his do well agree;
As touching all godliness a fool he was,
But in filthy demeanor who was worse?
Out of doubt in sin he did so excel and pass   1455

1427. *want*] lack, need.
1427. *witty page*] witty servant. There is perhaps a reflection of classical comedy here; cf. John Lyly's use of pages in his plays.
1434. *seen*] versed in, trained in.
1448. *conceit*] judgment, whim.

That the whole country for him God did curse.

IGNORANCE.

Leave, I pray you, sirs! what needeth this clatter?
You talk, sir, methink, you wot not what.
I pray you, go forward with our matter;
If you know any ways for our master's profit, speak that.   1460

CRUELTY.

To provide things to come by policy,
I will work under such a pretense
That all things shall appear honestly;
And for that cause am I named Prudence.
Again in providing your necessaries,   1465
I will in such a sort canvas the law
That such as be your adversaries
Shall be brought to Coram and awe.

MOROS.

O who hath such servants as I have,
So learned, so wise, in hall and in school?   1470
Among them all there is not one knave,
So that it skilleth not though I be a fool.
Would to God I had my servants together—
Pastime, Pleasure, and Robin-hood.
I pray you, take pain to call them hither;   1475
To have them wait on me, it should do me good.

IMPIETY.

You know the names of all your servants.
It may please you them here to recite.
We must also know the names of your tenants
That in your books of accounts we may them write.   1480

MOROS.

Pild-lousy Boy, you are the best;
None of them better than you, none so good.
Fip-pence and Tandidity be next,
Pastime, Pleasure, and Robin-hood.
Here be six honest persons indeed;   1485

1468. *brought to Coram*] brought before a judge. *Coram* (i.e., quorum) was the title of certain justices whose presence was necessary to constitute a bench.
1472. *it skilleth*] it matters.

By Saint Malkin, it is an honest train.
You shall have all one livery and weed,
For you all intend my profit and gain.

CRUELTY.

To the draper I will go and buy cloth
And array all your servants in a livery.   1490
To wait on you otherwise I would be loath;
That will be gentlemanlike, verily.

IMPIETY.

The great affairs I do consider
That Prudence in other things must have;
It is best, therefore, that we go together,   1495
So shall we be sure money to save.
And here we leave ancient Antiquity,
A person that no bad counsel will give;
He is prudent and full of sagacity;
His counsel see that you do believe.   1500

MOROS.

I have servants that finely can sing;
Let me hear, I pray you, what you can do.
Singing and playing I love above all thing;
Let me hear you, I pray you, go to.

IGNORANCE.

I am old and my voice is rusty,   1505
Yet I will sing to do you pleasure.

MOROS.

We will have drink if you be thirsty,
For I love to drink without measure.

IGNORANCE.

You must begin for I can no skill,
Yet I will jumble on as well as I can.   1510

CRUELTY.

We are indifferent, sing what ye will;
We were brought up with a singing man.

1486. *Saint Malkin*] The name "Malkin" was applied to a woman of the lower classes, often pejoratively to refer to a slattern or a drab; here, the canonization is comically appropriate.

1510. *jumble*] sing discordantly, to make a confused, rumbling noise.

Sing some merry song.

IMPIETY.

We take our leave of you for this season;
In time we shall wait on you again.

CRUELTY.

To have a time it standeth with reason,   1515
An order to set among your train.

MOROS.

In my house you will appoint me officers
Such as shall bring in to make frolic cheer;
But those that of Discipline and Piety are followers,
I would have rooted out both far and near.   1520
Fare ye well. As soon as you can return,
For I can do nothing without your counsel.

IMPIETY.

He that speaketh one word against you, we will burn,
Hang or head him like a rebel.   *Go out both.*

MOROS.

Yea marry, sir, this doth me good at the heart.   1525
Fare ye well, worthy to serve a gentleman.

IGNORANCE.

I tell you they were not brought up at the cart,
Full worshipfully their curtsey they can.
Now Sir, tell me how feel you your stomach?
Are you disposed to play, eat, or drink?   1530
Tell me if there be anything that you lack?
Devise what ye will, and in mind do ye think,
You shall have it whatsoever it doth cost.
We will neither pass of wind nor weather.

MOROS.

By my troth, the thing that I desire most   1535
Is in my cap to have a goodly feather.

1512.1.] *Q prints in the margin to the*   1516. An] *this edn.*; n *Q*, In *Brandl.*
left of ll. 1514–1515.

1515. *To ... time*] to appoint a time.
1527. *at the cart*] perhaps the cart used for public exposure and chastisement; cf. the phrase "whipping at cart's tail" (*OED*).
1529. *how ... stomach*] "what is your inclination?"
1534. *pass of*] care for, regard.
1536. *feather*] The feather is a conventional device to characterize the gallant; if the episode reveals Moros' folly, it also satirizes Elizabethan sartorial extravagances.

IGNORANCE.

    A feather? a matter of great importance.
    You shall have a feather if it cost a pound.
    Look up lustily, use a gentleman's countenance,
    And a feather, I trow, for you shall be found.   1540

MOROS.

    A feather would make me look aloft.
    Have you one? what, a red one?
    Now I thank you, it is goodly stuffed.
    This will make me a gentleman alone.
    Make it fast, I pray you, in my cap;   1545
    Now, by my honor, I thank you heartily,
    This will bear away a good rap.
    As good as a sallet for me verily,
    I look upward now alway still.
    God's days! my feather I cannot see.   1550
    Of this feather I can no skill.

       Look upward to see the feather. Stumble and fall.

    Beshrew thy heart, I have hurt my knee.

IGNORANCE.

    Like the philosopher that looked so high
    So long that he fell into the mire.
    Also another that gazed so into the sky,   1555
    Till he fell grovelinges in the fire.
    For a gentleman to look high it is meet,
    But in all things there is a mean;
    It becometh you to take heed to your feet
    Less you make your garments foul and unclean.   1560

MOROS.

    A vengeance take this foolish feather.

1543. stuffed] *this edn.*; stoft *Q,*   *left of ll. 1553–1556.*
Brandl.   1553. S.P. IGNORANCE] *Brandl; not in*
1551.1] *Q prints in the margin to the*   *Q.*

    1543. *stuffed*] trimmed, from "stow" V2 (*OED*).
    1547. *bear away*] withstand, endure.
    1548. *sallet*] light helmet or headpiece without crest.
    1553. *philosopher*] probably Thales; cf. Plato's *Theaetetus*, but the story
appears in Aesop's *Fables* and is applied to an astronomer. Such allusions
are common in the Renaissance and seem to have generic rather than
particular significance.
    1556. *grovelinges*] prostrate.

While it is there, I cannot look down.
IGNORANCE.

Fie, fie, you should have said so rather.
Look here, how unseemly you wear your gear.
See, see, it hangeth all on the one side,   1565
And your sword is between your legs.
Wise men will you mock and deride,
And not set by you a couple of eggs;
Let me help you to set your gown right.
On this fashion your sword you must wear.   1570
Alack, alack, if I had a good sight,
I would trim you in your gear.
MOROS.

Must I not look over my shoulder some time?
I have seen some that thus would jet.
IGNORANCE.

To be equal with the best do you cline.   1575
Remember still that in honor you are set.

Here enter'th Discipline.

DISCIPLINE.

The longer thou livest, the more fool thou art,
Every day more fool than other.
Thou wilt play such a foolish part
As shall shame country, father and mother.—   1580
Good audience, note this fool's proceeding.
In tender age, in Idleness he was nuzzled.
In adolency, when pubes was springing,
Touching virtue as a dog that is muzzled,
Ill-willing to learn and therefore unapt,   1585
All his senses he applied to vice;
Anon with such companions he was wrapt,
As no young man will be that is wise.
Never could I bring him to Piety,

1583. springing] *Brandl*; ſpringing
Q.

1563. *rather*] sooner.
1574. *jet*] swagger, strut.
1575. *cline*] incline (perhaps aphetic form).
1583. *pubes*] pubic hair.

That is God to serve, to love, to fear;   1590
Neither to do ought for his own utility,
Neither reverence in his heart to bear,
But as fools all are unpatient,
So was he given to hastiness and ire.
In lechery as fools be all incontinent,   1595
Through Idleness he was set on fire.
When to man's state once he attained,
Worldly Fortune did him in wealth erect;
God and good counsel he disdained,
Being then with all misery infect.   1600
Now is he come unto plain Impiety
Which persuadeth him God to deny;
And with him is joined Crudelity
Against the innocents to reply.
Behold here he is led with Ignorance   1605
So that he will not believe the verity.
Beside these he hath other maintenance
To uphold him in his iniquity.
Of such the Prophet did prophesy,
The fool saith in his heart there is no God.   1610
Corrupt are they and full of villainy;
Therefore, shall they be beat with an iron rod.

MOROS.

Can you tell of whom this tale they have told?
I am a man; he knoweth me not now.

IGNORANCE.

Tush, face him out. Fear not, be bold,   1615
For all this talk he hath of you.

MOROS.

Sirrah, shall I draw my sword or dagger?
Is it not best to kill him out of hand?

IGNORANCE.

Tush, you are but a craking bragger;
I would see you boldly him to withstand.   1620

1618. Is it] *this edn.*; It is *Q,*
Brandl.

1609. *the Prophet*] Psalm 14:1.
1619. *craking*] boasting, bragging.

MOROS.

>Would to God that Pild-lousy Boy were here.
>Good Lord, what meaneth my man Robin-hood?

IGNORANCE.

>Are you afraid? For very shame, draw near.
>I would let out some of his saucy blood.

MOROS.

>Good man, you, know you who I am? 1625
>My beard is grown, I am a man now.
>You shall repent that hither you came;
>I will kill you, I make God a vow.
>A vengeance on it, my dagger will not out.
>Sir, I pray you, how my hand doth quake. 1630
>Rail on me, you beggarly lout?
>You and I a fray will make;
>Am I not a gentleman, knave?
>Body of God, will you presume?
>Truly, Tandidity, no power I have 1635
>So great is my anger and fume.

DISCIPLINE.

>A fool uttereth his anger in haste,
>And hath not the wit measure to keep;
>Where much anger is, strength is past,
>And wisdom is drowned in folly deep. 1640
>As fair legs to a cripple are unseemly,
>So to a fool honor is undecent;
>As snow in harvest is untimely,
>So is it a plague where a fool is regent.
>What should a fool do with money or treasure, 1645
>Seeing that sapience he cannot buy?
>In voluptuousness he walloweth without measure,
>As a beastly swine doth in his filthy sty.

MOROS.

>Body of God, for anger I am like to die.
>Where is Robin-hood and Pild-lousy Boy? 1650

1632. a fray] *Brandl*; afray *Q*.

1636. *fume*] fit of anger.
1637–1640.] Prov. 26:1 and 7.
1644. *regent*] ruler.

Callest thou me fool? I utterly thee defy;
Thee and all thine, this sword shall utterly destroy.
Pluck out my sword, good Tandidity;
Passion of God, kill him downright.

IGNORANCE.

He should not long live in tranquillity   1655
If I had my perfect senses and sight;
But be you ruled by my counsel,
For this time let us depart and give place.
We shall send them hither that shall him compel
To hold his peace, yea, spite of his face.   1660

MOROS.

Content, content. We will go hence indeed.—
We will send to you ere it be long.—
Alas, where be my servants in time of need?
This tough whoreson for me is too strong.   *Go out both.*

DISCIPLINE.

As Scripture calleth this the highest sapience   1665
God to know, to fear, to love, and obey,
And the most pure and high intelligence
Is to follow his precepts night and day;
So God to contemn, to despise, to hate
Is such a folly as none is more extreme.   1670
This is the most miserable state,
Yea, no state at all as wise men do esteem.
When a fool is compassed with impiety,
Which is the contempt of God and his ordinances,
And such a fool erected to authority,   1675
The people must needs sustain many grievances,
For there God cannot be duly honored,
His holy sacraments had in estimation,
Neither the public weal rightly governed,
But all cometh to utter dissipation.   1680
If we should say all that might be said
Of fools in their extreme folly,
How God's people by them have decayed,

1670. more] *Brandl*; mere *Q*.

1665. *Scripture*] Prov. 1:1 ff.
1669. *contemn*] scorn.

Two days would not serve, I think, truly.   *Go out.*

Here enter'th People.

PEOPLE.

Intollerabilius nil est quam dives avarus,   1685
Quam stultus locuples, quam Fortunatus iniquus.
There is nothing more intolerable
Than a rich man that is covetous,
A fool wealthy, a wicked man fortunable,
A judge partial, an old man lecherous.   1690
Good Lord, how are we now molested.
The devil hath sent one into our country,
A monster whom God and man hath detested,
A fool that came up from a low degree.
My name is People, for I represent   1695
All the people where Moros doth dwell,
Such a person as is with nothing content
So that we think him to be a devil of hell.
Neither learning, wisdom nor reason
Will serve where he taketh opinion;   1700
His words and acts be all out of season.
By honest men he setteth not an onion
And, as he is, such is his family;
Not one honest person among them I do know,
Ruffians, villains, swearers full of blasphemy,   1705
Despisers of all honest men, both high and low.
A whole alphabet of his officers
I can recite though it be not in order,
A rabble of roisterly rufflers
Which trouble all honest men in our borders.   1710
As for Impiety, Cruelty, and Ignorance,
Are chief of his council, verily;
Idleness, Wrath, and lecherous dalliance
Are they which in youth kept him company.
Sir Anthony Arrogant, auditor,   1715

1697. as is] Q; as this is *Brandl.*

1709. *rufflers*] swaggerers, but the term was also applied to a class of
vagabonds who posed as former servants.

1711. *As for*] with respect to; the subject of the clause is an ellipted
"they" and the clause is parallel to that in ll. 1713–1714.

Bartolmew Briber, bailie,
Clement Catchpole, cofferer,
Division Double-faced Davy,
Edmund Envious, chief of the ewery,
Fabian Falsehood, his head farmer,   1720
Gregory Gorbelly, the gouty,
Governeth the grain in the garner,
Hans Hazarder the horsekeeper is,
James the just is the chief judge,
Leonard Lecherous is man of law, Iwis,   1725
Kenolm the knave is in cookery no drudge,
Martin the murderer, master of music,
Nicol Never-thrift, the notary,
Owen Overwhart, master in physic,
Quintine the quaffer, for nothing necessary,   1730
Rafe Ruffian, the rude railer,
Steven Sturdy, master surveyor,
Thomas the thief, his chief tailor,
William Witless, the great warrior,
With these and such like many moe,   1735
We in his circuit be oppressed;
For remedy we wot not whither to go
To have our calamity redressed.
Unto God only we refer our cause;
Humbly we commit all to his judgment,   1740
We have offended him and his holy laws;
Therefore, are we worthy of this punishment.   *Go out.*

        Enter [Moros] *furiously with a grey beard.*

MOROS.
   Where is he? Blood, sides, heart and wounds!

1742.1.] *Q prints in left margin*
beneath S.P. opposite ll. 1744–1747.

_____

   1716. *bailie*] another form of "bailiff," the steward who collects rents and
manages the estate.
   1717. *Catchpole*] tax-gatherer, a warrant officer who arrests for debt.
   1717. *cofferer*] treasurer; but also one who makes coffins.
   1718. *Division*] perhaps used here in the sense of one who causes division.
   1719. *ewery*] the apartment where ewers of water and table linen were
stored.
   1721. *Gorbelly*] protuberant belly.

A man I am now, every inch of me.
I shall teach the knave to keep his bounds; 1745
What his prattling will profit I will see.
With me to come I would not suffer one:
Yet servants I have and that plenty.
I myself, I trow, am good enough alone,
Yea, by the mass, if there were twenty. 1750
Make no more ado but fend thy head.
Have at thee. Thou shalt know that I am a man.

Fight alone.

I will make thee that thou shalt eat no more bread,
Rail no more at Master Moros then.
What there? Either I have him slain 1755
Or else from my sight he is fled.
He is never like to trouble me again;
I warrant him, I have brought him in bed.

Enter [God's Judgment] *with a terrible visure.*

GOD'S JUDGMENT.

The longer thou livest, the more fool thou art.
This to thee hath been often recited; 1760
For so much as thou hast play'd such a fool's part,
As a fool thou shalt be justly requited.
I represent God's severe judgment,
Which dallieth not where to strike he doth purpose.
Hither am I sent to the punishment 1765
Of this impious fool, here called Moros
Who hath said there is no God in his heart.
His holy laws he has stoutly blasphemed,
Godly Discipline could never his mind convert,
Virtue nor honesty are not of him esteemed. 1770

MOROS.

A pestilence take them, whoreson knaves!
They are ever absent when I have need.

1752.1.] *Q prints in left margin*   S.P. *opposite ll. 1756–1758.*
opposite l. 1753.   1768. has] *this edn.;* had *Q, Brandl.*
1758.1.] *Q prints in left margin above*

1758.1. *visure*] vizor or mask; appearance.
1767.] Psalm 14:1.

Whoresons, bring your clubs, bills, bows and staves.
I see that it is time now to take heed.

GOD'S JUDGMENT.

According unto his most wicked belief,   1775
So with his neighbors wickedly he dealeth;
From the poor he doth take and nothing doth give,
He oppresseth, bribeth, defraudeth, and stealeth.
If he believed God good works to reward
And devil's wickedness to punish in fire,   1780
His promises and threats he would more regard,
Do penance and for mercy desire;
But such fools in their hearts do say
That there is no God, neither heaven nor hell.
According to their saying they follow that way   1785
Like as a little before I did tell.
For as much as vengeance to God doth belong
And he will the same recompense,
That he is a God of power, mighty and strong,
The fools shall know by experience.   1790
With this sword of vengeance I strike thee.

Strike Moros *and let him fall down.*

Thy wicked household shall be dispersed,
Thy children shall be rooted out to the fourth degree
Like as the mouth of God hath rehearsed.

MOROS.

Either I have the falling sickness,   1795
Or else with the palsy I am stricken.
I feel in myself no manner of quickness;
I begin now strangely to sicken.

GOD'S JUDGMENT.

If thou hast grace for mercy now call,
Yet thy soul perchance thou mayst save;   1800
For his mercy is above his works all,
On penitent sinners he is wont mercy to have.

1791.1.] Q *prints in margin to the left*
of ll. 1792–1794.

1793. *fourth degree*] fourth generation; the reference is ultimately to
Exodus 20:5 and the second of the Ten Commandments.
1797. *quickness*] life.

MOROS.

> It was but a qualm came over my heart;
> I lack nothing but a cup of good wine.

GOD'S JUDGMENT.

> Indurate wretches can not convert   1805
> But die in their filthiness like swine.

Enter Confusion *with an ill-favored visure and all things beside ill-favored.*

> Behold, here cometh shame and confusion,
> The reward of such wicked fools all.
> To all the world shall appear thy abusion,
> Thy wickedness, and false belief to great and small.   1810

MOROS.

> Here is an ill-favored knave, by the mass.
> Get thee hence, thief, with a wanion.

GOD'S JUDGMENT.

> This is the reward of such a foolish ass;
> Forevermore he shall be thy companion.

CONFUSION.

> The wise shall have honor in possession,   1815
> Thus the wise King Solomon doth say,
> But the portion of fools is Confusion
> Which abideth with them forever and aye.

GOD'S JUDGMENT.

> Confusion spoil him of his array;
> Give him his fool's coat for him due;   1820
> His chain and his staff take thou away;
> In sorrow and care forever let him rue.

MOROS.

> Am I asleep, in a dream, or in a trance?
> Ever methink that I should be waking.
> Body of God! this is a wonderful chance;   1825
> I cannot stand on my feet for quaking.   [*Fall down.*]

1806.1.] *Q prints in margin to the left of*   1811.] *Q prints S.P. to the left of*
ll. 1806–1811.   *l. 1812.*

1809. abusion] perversion.

1812. with a wanion] with a vengeance or curse.

1815–1818.] possibly Prov. 3:35.

1820.] The change of clothes symbolizes Moros' final state; Moros is probably stripped of his finery to reveal the fool's clothing underneath.

CONFUSION.

 As the ears of an ass appeared in Midas,
 Though it were long ere it were known,
 So at length evermore it cometh to pass
 That the folly of fools is openly blown;   1830
 And then in this world they have confusion,
 That is reproof, derision, and open shame;
 And when they have ended all their abusion,
 They leave behind them an abominable name.
 Come, foolish Moros, come go with me,   1835
 And I shall bring thee to a shameful end.
 Thy malice will not let thee thy folly to see
 So that thou hast not the grace thy life to amend.

MOROS.

 Sancti, Amen. Where is my goodly gear?
 I see well that I was asleep indeed.   1840
 What, am I fain a fool's coat to wear?
 We must learn at "Christ's cross me speed."
 Other I was a gentleman and had servants,
 Or else I dreamed that I was a gentleman.

CONFUSION.

 But thou art now a peasant of all peasants,   1845
 A derision and mock to man and woman.
 Come forth of thy folly to receive thy hire,
 Confusion, poverty, sickness and punishment;
 And after this life, eternal fire
 Due for fools that be impenitent.   1850

MOROS.

 Go with thee, ill-favored knave?
 I had lever thou wert hanged by the neck.
 If it please the devil me to have
 Let him carry me away on his back.

1828. ere] er *Q*; or *Brandl.*

 1827. *ears . . . Midas*] In the musical contest between Apollo and Pan, Midas sided with Pan; as punishment Apollo changed Midas' ears into ass' ears which Midas tried to hide (Ovid. *Meta.*, XI, 145 ff.).
 1841. *fain*] obliged.
 1842. *learn at*] idiomatically, "to acquire knowledge."
 1842. *Christ's . . . speed*] cf. l. 471.
 1843. *Other*] either.

CONFUSION.

I will carry thee to the devil indeed;   1855
The world shall be well rid of a fool.

MOROS.

A due to the devil? God send us good speed.
Another while with the devil I must go to school.

[*Exit* Moros *on* Confusion's *back.*]

GOD'S JUDGMENT.

For sin, though God suffer'th impiety
Greatly to the dishonor of his name,   1860
Yet at length he throweth down iniquity
And putteth the authors thereof to shame.
So confounded he tyrants in times past
Whom holy scripture fools doth call;
For as beasts here their times they did waste,   1865
And from one wickedness to another did fall.
What shall we need their names to recite,
Seeing that every man hath of them heard?
In our times we have known fools full of spite,
And in this world have seen their reward.   1870
We do not only them fools call here
Which have not the perfect use of reason,
Innocents whereof be many far and near
In whom discretion is geason,
But those are the greatest fools properly   1875
Which disdain to learn sapience
To speak, to do, to work all things orderly
And as God hath given intelligence;
But contrary to nature and God's will
They stop their eyes through wilful ignorance,   1880
They seek to slay, to prison, to poll, to pill
Only for their own furtherance.
Of all fools indeed this is the worst kind,
Whereof this time we have treated,
Which to all mischief giveth his mind   1885

1866. one] *this edn.*; our *Q, Brandl.*

1857. *due*] debt; cf. "to give the devil his due."
1857. *speed*] success.
1874. *geason*] scanty.

And refuseth to be instructed.
Many things moe of fools we could talk,
But we have detained long our audience;
Another way I am compelled to walk,
Desiring you awhile to have patience.   1890

Go out.

Enter all iii [, Discipline, Piety, *and* Exercitation].

EXERCITATION.

Although this fool of whom we have spoken
Hath refused all honest exercise,
Yet the hearts of wise men God doth open,
Virtuous occupation not to despise;
For undoubtedly it is as hard as they say   1895
To get the scepter out of the hand of Hercules,
As for one to be well-occupied night or day
That is nuzzled in unhappy idleness.
For as Theophylactus doth write,
Idleness hath taught all iniquity;   1900
And as Ezekiel also doth recite,
Idleness taught the Sodomites impiety.
Never will I believe that man good to be,
Whether he be of the clergy or lay,
Whom idle and not well-occupied I see,   1905
Which do nothing but eat, drink, and play.

PIETY.

We desire no man here to be offended
In that we use this term "piety"
Which is despised and vilely pended
Of sinners and authors of iniquity;   1910
For the heathen philosophers and orators
Used the same term and in the same sense
As learned Christians, true worshippers

1890.2.] *Q prints in left margin*   1913. As learned] *this edn.*; Learned
opposite l. 1890.   Q, Brandl.

1899. *Theophylactus*] fourth-century archbishop of Achrida (Bulgaria)
whose commentaries on the New Testament and the minor prophets were
popular in the sixteenth century.
1901.] Ezekiel 16:48–50.
1909. *pended*] confined.

Created of piety with his science.
Plato, Aristotle, Valerius, and Tully   1915
Wrote of piety, and diverse other,
And called it an honor due to God only,
And a natural duty to father and mother.
Saint Augustine in his book of God's city,
And in other noble works that he did make,   1920
Treateth holily of this term piety;
And as he doth take it so do we take it:
Ipsa est illa sapientia quae Pietas vocatur,
Qua colitur pater luminum:
A quo est omne datum optimum.   1925
That is, the highest sapience notified,
Which is called piety indeed,
Whereby the Father of light is worshipped
From whom every good gift doth proceed.

DISCIPLINE.

Touching my person called Discipline,   1930
In the process I have said sufficient;
Yet to end with some honest doctrine,
You shall hear a learned man's judgment.
There be many disciplines as authors do say;
Among all, there be two principal,   1935
That be *Scire* and *Sapere* alway,
To have cunning and wisdom withal.

EXERCITATION.

Ut furiosus habens gladium, sic doctus iniquus.
Without fail this is a notable verse;
I would all men could it well by rote.   1940
The sentence thereof Solomon doth rehearse,
I wish all the audience it to note.
A wicked man having learning and cunning
And doth many sciences understand

1938. *furiosus*] Brandl; *fluuiosus* Q.

1936. *Scire and Sapere*] The distinction between the Latin verbs is sug-
gested in their derivatives "science" and "sapience"; *scire* means "to
know," "to be skilled in" (cf. l. 1937 "to have cunning") while *sapere*
means "to taste" or "to have discernment."
1941. *Solomon*] perhaps Prov. 26:18.

Is like one whose wits are running,   1945
I mean a mad man having a sword in his hand.
PIETY.
    For as a mad man having in his hand edge-tool
Seeketh both himself and other to kill,
So a cunning man without wisdom is but a fool,
For both himself and many other he doth spill.   1950
Wherefore whosoever hath intelligence
Let him humbly desire of God evermore
That he will also give him sapience
To bestow his cunning to his honor.
DISCIPLINE.
    This is the sum of the whole intent,   1955
To induce youth to these two aforesaid,
Scire and *Sapere*, you know what is meant.
Then many things amiss shall be well-stayed.
EXERCITATION.
    To learn many things and many things to know,
Then to have wisdom the same to direct,   1960
These be two disciplines, meet for high and low,
Which to all virtues do the mind erect.
PIETY.
    For this time we have said sufficient;
With *Scire* and *Sapere* we make an end,
Beseeching our Lord God omnipotent   1965
That among us his grace he may send.
DISCIPLINE.
    And here we make an end, trusting that all you present
Will bear us record that no estate we defame;
To praise the good order now set is our intent,
And to further the glory of God's holy name.   1970
EXERCITATION.
    God save the Queen's Highness and the nobility,
Defend her long we beseech thee, Lord;

1947. For as a] *Brandl*; For a *Q*.

  1958. *well-stayed*] well-supported.
  1969. *good order*] The "good order" is that established by Elizabeth, although there may be a more immediate reference to the Statute of Artificers (1563) and a hope for a more stable economic order.

Which is the patroness of all humility,
A setter-forth of truth, and lover of concord.

PIETY.

God preserve the Queen's most honorable Council, 1975
With all the Magistrates of this region,
That they may agree to maintain God's Gospel
Which is the most true and sincere religion.
To root out Anti-Christ, I pray God, they may take pain;
Then will the Lord send them honor and fame 1980
And, after this life, give them the reward of the same.

DISCIPLINE.

Pray we for the clergy and whole spirituality,
That they may teach and set forth God's truth alway;
I beseech you, let us pray for the whole commonality,
That upon us all God mercy take may, 1985
So that each one of us in the right way may stay.
All glory, honor, empery, majesty, and dignity
Be given both now and evermore to the blessed Trinity.

FINIS

1979. pain] *Q. (Brandl suggests that*   *merely an error in rhyming.)*
a line is lost, but more probably there is

1976. *this region*] If the choice of "region" is not dictated by rhyme, the
word's vagueness is appropriate for a play performed by a traveling company.

ENOUGH IS AS GOOD AS A FEAST

Seven may easily play this interlude

THE NAMES OF THE PLAYERS

WORLDLY MAN: *for one*

PROLOGUE ⎫ *for one*   5
HEAVENLY MAN ⎭

CONTENTATION ⎫
TEMERITY [*alias* AGILITY] ⎪
IGNORANCE [*alias* DEVOTION *or* SIR NICHOLAS, ⎬ *for one*
    a priest] ⎪   10
SATAN ⎭

ENOUGH ⎫ *for one*
HIRELING ⎭

INCONSIDERATION [*alias* REASON] ⎫   15
SERVANT [*to the Worldly Man*] ⎪
REST ⎬ *for one*
PROPHET ⎭

PRECIPITATION [*alias* READY WIT] ⎫   20
TENANT ⎪
[GOD'S] PLAGUE ⎬ *for one*
PHYSICIAN [MASTER FLEBISHITEN] ⎭

COVETOUSNESS THE VICE [*alias* POLICY]: *for another*   25

1–2.] The title page lists the characters in terms of the casting. As Craik points out, the action is thrice held up for costume changes (ll. 280, 1427, and 1471). A slight revision could prevent these interruptions: for actor three Contentation, Servant, Prophet; for actor four Temerity, Satan, Rest; for actor five Inconsideration, Enough, Hireling, Ignorance (Craik, pp. 34–35 and 131; the line numbering is that of the present edition).

7. *Contentation*] Contentment; cf. Heywood (1570) "Let contentashyn be decree, Make virtue of necessytee" (*OED*).

8. *Temerity*] rashness.

24. *Flebishiten*] i.e., "flea-be-shitten."

25. *Covetousness*] In *Enough* the adjectival form "covetous" is regularly used for the more normal substantive form "covetise" (cf., however, ll. 296, 581, and 589); the form "covetousness" occurs only on the title page.

A Comedy or Interlude Entitled

Enough Is as Good as a Feast

Very Fruitful, Godly and Full of Pleasant Mirth
Compiled by W. Wager

PROLOGUE

I know that this worshipful audience
Is at this time together congregate
Of our practice to have intelligence
And with the same themselves to recreate.
God grant us grace the same well to publicate.   5
But for them that have slept at Parnassus
This faculty is more meet for them than for us;
Pandite pierides vestro sacra ostia vitae.
Open your holy doors O pleasant Muses;
Direct our tongues to speak eloquently,   10
Virtues to praise and to touch abuses,
Dividing either of them plain and directly
That it may appear to all our audience evidently
That this matter which we now go about
By your inspiration was first found out.   15
O that with some grace you would us inspire

0.5. PROLOGUE] *this edn.*; Pro-   8   *vitae*] *this edn.*; vita *Q*.
logus *Q*.

---

2. *congregate*] assembled.
3. *intelligence*] understanding.
8. *Pandite . . . vitae*] cf. l. 9; Latin tags which are translated in text are
not glossed. The Latin line is not included in the metrical pattern of the
stanza.
12. *Dividing*] distinguishing.

And deal with us as with Orpheus you dealt;
Then should all affections have their desire,
For through his music he made stones to melt.
No kind of pain in hell then the souls felt,   20
For he played so pleasantly with his harp
That they forgot their pains grievous and sharp.
Tantalus forgot his hunger and thirst;
Sisyphus left off rolling his stone;
Ixion, tormented among the worst,   25
Forgot his wheel that he was hanged on;
The women Belides left work anon
Whose labor was continually to fill a tun
Whereout by clefts the liquor still doth run.
These fables wherefore do I call to mind?   30
Truly because I desire with all my heart
That our English meter may be of such kind,
Both to leave all grievousness and smart
And also to be pleasant in every part,

27. women] *this edn.*; woman *Q*.

---

17. *Orpheus*] The Muses taught Orpheus to use the harp which Apollo gave him; and he "dyd with his musike delyte wylde beastes and infernall spirites, and moued stones with his sweete harmonie; whereby he recouered his wife Euryduce out of hel" (Cooper).

18. *affections*] passions.

23. *Tantalus*] For betraying the counsel of the gods, Tantalus is tortured in hell by standing in a river from which he can never drink and reaching for fruit which is unattainable.

24. *Sisyphus*] "a great thief, which was slayne by Theseus, of whom it is feyned, that in hell he turneth a stone up to a great hyll toppe: but when it is at the toppe, it falleth downe againe, and reneweth his labour" (Cooper).

25. *Ixion*] For boasting of an affair with Juno, "he was driuen downe into hel and there bounde to a wheele alwaies tournynge and full of serpentes . . ." (Cooper).

27. *Belides*] The fifty nieces of Belus and daughters of Danaus who, with the exception of Hypermnestra, murdered their husbands on their wedding night to evade the prophecy of the oracle that Danaus would be killed by a husband of his daughter. As punishment the daughters were put to "this continual labour, to fill with water a greate tunne [barrel] full of holes, so that it ranne out faster than they coulde poure it in" (Cooper).

29. *still*] always.

32. *meter*] composition "in meter," verse.

That those which come for recreation   35
May not be void of their expectation.
Foets feigned Mercurius to have wings,
Both on his head and on his heels also,
For lively and swift he was in all things,
Appearing rather to flee than to go;   40
Of him they feign many goodly things mo.
But for our purpose this shall serve this season
And why I speak you shall know the reason.
Mercurius is the god of eloquence,
By whom I understand the ministers of talk;   45
Such must have the wings of intelligence
In their heads before their tongues too far do walk.
The danger of rash speech they must wisely calk.
When, where, and to whom they speak they must note
Before that anything pass out of their throat.   50
As Mercurius hath wings upon his head
So hath he wings on his heels ready to fly;
When affections standeth in reason's stead,
Reporters of tales use eftsoons to lie:
The heels affections do also signify.   55
The wings do always reason comprehend
Which unto virtue ought to condescend.
Few words to wise men are sufficient;
Without a cause I give not this monition.
Unto good men it is plain and evident   60
That many men have that lewd condition
By their evil words to bring good men into suspicion;
By their undiscreet talk they do much harm

37–57. *Mercurius*] "the sonne of Iupiter by Maia, whome the poetes
faigne to haue wynges in his head and feete, to signifie, that talke (which is
represented by the person of Mercurie) doth quickly passe through the
ayer . . . . He was coumpted the God of eloquence" (Cooper). In the
second illustration of S. Batman's *The Trauayled Pylgrime, Bringing News from
All Partes of the Worlde* (1569), the allegorical figure Thought is represented
with wings.

45. *understand*] mean.   48. *calk*] calculate, reckon.
54. *eftsoons*] often.   56. *comprehend*] represent.
59. *monition*] warning.   61. *lewd*] unprincipled.
63. *undiscreet*] indiscreet.

Because they want reason their tongues to charm.
Let this pass and go we to the argument   65
Which we will declare in words general.
Now such as have a learned judgment
Know that among the poets comical
In brief sentence it was usual
To show the whole contents of the comedy   70
In the argument, which did well verily.
But our tongues hath not so comely a grace
In that point, as hath the Latin and Greek;
We cannot like them our sentences eloquently place
That our poets to their orators may be like   75
As they know well which for such matters do seek.
But to do our best indeed we will not neglect
Trusting that wise men the same will accept.
Our title is *Enough is as good as a feast*
Which rhetorically we shall amplify   80
So that it shall appear both to most and least
That our meaning is but honesty;
Yet now and then we will dally merrily.
So we shall please them that of mirth be desirous,
For we play not to please them that be curious.   85
For a preface I fear I am too long
But I have said that I will say now,
The Worldly Man is frolic, lusty and strong

---

68. *poets comical*] Plautus and Terence.

69. *sentence*] While the term may mean "pointed sayings, aphorism," the word also is used to refer to a "passage, an indefinite portion of discourse or writing." In the present instance the reference would seem to be to the short arguments which summarize the plot and which precede the Prologues to classical comedies. The subsequent references to the limitations of the English language recall Ascham's praise of Terence in *The Schoolmaster*: "his wordes be chosen so purelie, placed so orderlie, and all his stuff so neetlie packed up and wittilie compassed in every place ..." (*Works*, ed. Wright [Cambridge, 1904], p. 287).

75. *like*] The *OED* spelling "leeke" suggests a pronunciation which would justify the rhyme with "seek." Here as elsewhere, rhymes may be accurate although dependent upon phonetic shifts or dialectal pronunciations; cf. H. C. Wyld, *Studies in English Rhymes from Surrey to Pope* (London, 1923).

82. *honesty*] decency, decorum.   88. *frolic*] sportive, merry.

Who will show his qualities before you;
Stout he is and in any wise will not bow.   90
Behold, yonder he cometh into this place;
Therefore, thus I finish our simple preface.

Enter Worldly Man *stout and frolic.*

WORLDLY MAN.

Because I am a man endued with treasure,
Therefore a worldly man men do me call;
Indeed I have riches and money at my pleasure,   95
Yea, and I will have more in spite of them all.
A common saying, better is envy than ruth;
I had rather they should spite than pity me,
For the old saying nowadays proveth truth:
Nought have, nought set by, as daily we see.   100
Iwis, I am not of the mind as some men are
Which look for no more than will serve necessity;
No, against a day to come I do prepare,
That when age cometh I may live merrily.
"O," saith one, "enough is as good as a feast."   105
Yea, but who can tell what his end shall be?
Therefore, I count him worse than a beast
That will not have that in respect and see
As by mine own father an example I may take.
He was beloved of all men and kept a good house   110
Whilst riches lasted, but when that did slake,
There was no man that did set by him a louse.
And so at such time as he from the world went,
I mean when he died, he was not worth a groat;
And they that all his substance had spent   115

92.] *after this line Q prints* "Finis."   115. substance] *this edn.*; snbstance
centered above a bar design.   Q.
113. as] *this edn.*; as as Q.

90. *wise*] manner, way.
100. *Nought . . . by*] allied to the proverbial "nothing have, nothing
crave" (Tilley, N 291).
101. *Iwis*] certainly, truly.
108. *in . . . see*] in consideration; i.e., to keep his end in mind.
111. *slake*] diminish, fall off.
112. *set by*] esteem.

For the value of twelve pence would have cut his throat.
But I trow I will take heed of such;
They shall go, ere they drink when they come to me.
It doth me good to tell the chinks in my hutch
More than at the tavern or ale house to be.   120

[*Enter* Heavenly Man *and* Contentation.]

HEAVENLY MAN.

God careth for his, as the prophet David doth say,
And preserveth them under his merciful wing—
The heavenly I mean, that his will do obey
And observe his holy commandments in all thing;
Yet not for our sakes, nor for our deserving,   125
But for his own namesake openly to declare
That all men here on earth ought to live in his fear.

WORLDLY MAN [*aside*].

This same is one of our jolly talkers
That prattleth so much of heaven and hell.
O, I tell you these are goodly walkers,   130
Of many strange things they can tell.
They pass men, yea angels they excel.—
Sir, are you not called the Heavenly Man?
I have been in your company ere now but I cannot tell when.

HEAVENLY MAN.

Yes certainly sir, that is my name,   135
Unworthy of any such title I do confess;
God grant that I may deserve the same
And that my faults I may amend and redress.
Therefore now the truth do you here express,
Is not the Worldly Man your name?   140

WORLDLY MAN.

Yea indeed sir, I am the very same.

CONTENTATION.

From the Heavenly Man I cannot be long absent
Which in God's promises hath his consolation,
Considering that he always is content

---

119. *It . . . good*] it pleases me.
119. *tell . . . hutch*] count the money in my coffer.
121. *prophet David*] probably Psalm 91:4.

−87−

Patiently to suffer God's visitation.   145
For understand you, my name is Contentation
Whom the Worldly Man doth mock and deride
And will not suffer him once in his mind to abide.

WORLDLY MAN [*aside*].

This same is the grandsire of them all,
This is he that will through water and fire.   150
Good reasoning betwixt us now hear you shall,
For to follow him he will me earnestly require;
But he shall be hanged or he have his desire.—
You are welcome sir, saving my quarrel indeed;
You have reported of me much more than you need.   155

CONTENTATION.

Nothing but truth sir, certainly I have said;
Oft times I have counseled you your covetousness to leave,
But my words as feathers in the wind you have weighed
And stuck to them as glue to the water doth cleave.
But take heed the reward thereof you shall receive;   160
Once again I advertize thee to be content
And give thanks to God for that he hath thee sent.

WORLDLY MAN.

I pray you be you content, for I am pleased,
And meddle you no more with me than I do with you.

HEAVENLY MAN.

To be angry without a cause, without mends, must be eased;   165
We will be more earnest than ever we were now.
Woe (saith our Savior) to those that are rich,

---

164. meddle you] *this edn.*; meddle   166. ever] *this edn.*; ener *Q.*
yon *Q.*   167. Savior] *this edn.*; Saniour *Q.*

---

150. *will*] elliptical construction; i.e., he will go through.

153. *or*] before.

158. *feathers . . . wind*] Tilley, F 162; the phrase "glue to water" in the next line is unrecorded as a proverb.

161. *advertize*] admonish.

165. *mends*] remedy.

165. *eased*] ceased.

167. *Woe . . . Savior*)] The reference is probably to Math. 6:19–21; the argument is a homilectic commonplace, cf. Tyndale, "Exposition of Math. v, vi, vii," *Expositions* (London, The Parker Society, 1849, XLIII, 103).

Which therein only have their consolation.
He curseth them not because they have much,
But because they receive it not with contentation,   170
Building therewith to themselves a good foundation,
That is to lay here on earth treasure great store
To purchase a kingdom that lasteth evermore.

WORLDLY MAN.

Passion of me, masters! what would you have me to do?
You are fond fellows indeed as ever I knew.   175
If I should not take pains, ride, run and go
For my living, what thereof would ensue?
A beggar should I die, masters this is true.
Then my wife and children that I leave behind,
I fear me at your hands small relief should find.   180

HEAVENLY MAN.

I have been young (saith David) and now am old,
Yet the righteous forsaken I never did see,
Nor their seed begging bread I did not behold;
Therefore, your mind to the prophets doth not agree.
Cast all thy burden and care (saith Christ) on me,   185
And I will provide to keep thee from danger and strife;
Only seek thou to live a godly and good life.

CONTENTATION.

When Solon was asked of Cressus the king,
What man was most happy in this vale terrestrial,
To the end he seemed to attribute that thing   190
When men be associate with treasures celestial.

WORLDLY MAN.

By the beginning no man can judge; the same Solon doth say
That any man is happy that beareth breath;

---

175. *fond*] foolish.   176. *go*] walk.
181–183.] Psalm 37:25.
185.] If the allusion is to Christ's words in Math. 11:28 ff. or Math.
6:25, the diction recalls Psalm 55:22: "O cast thy burthen, or care, upon
the Lorde, he shall noryshe the, and not leaue the ryghteous in unquyet-
nesse" (Bible, 1551).
188–191.] The source is ultimately Herodotus I, 50; cf. Painter's *Palace
of Pleasure* I, 7: "King Craesus of Lydia reasoneth with the wyseman Solon,
of the happie lyfe of man. Who little esteeming his good aduise, under-
stoode before his death, that no man (but by vertue) can in this life attain
felicitie."

But yet by the end partly judge we may,
For true happiness (saith he) consisteth after death.   195

HEAVENLY MAN.

If this be true as undoubtedly it is,
What men are more wicked, wretched and miserable
Than those that in riches account their bliss,
Being infected with ambition that sickness uncurable.

CONTENTATION.

The treasure of this world we may well compare   200
To Circe, the witch, with her crafty cautility
Wherewith many men's minds so poisoned are
That quite they are carried to all infidelity.
They are conjured so indeed and bewitched so sore
That treasure is their trust, yea, hope and delight.   205
Enough serveth them not till that they have more,
So against Contentation they still strive and fight.

HEAVENLY MAN.

Though the worldly man do follow their lust,
Crying, "On earth is our felicity and pleasure";
Yet God doth so rule the hearts of the just   210
That their study is chiefly to get heavenly treasure.

WORLDLY MAN.

Friends, I take you both for honest men,
I promise you I would be glad to do for the best;
Marry then, I take care which way and when
I may get treasure therewith to live in rest.   215
O, methinks it is a very pleasant thing
To see a great heap of old angels and crowns;
When I have store of money, I can be merry and sing,
For money, as men say, winneth both cities and towns.

HEAVENLY MAN.

Alas, why should you not have that in estimation   220
Which God hath prepared for his dear elect?

---

201. *Circe*] In the *Odyssey*, Circe transformed Odysseus' companions into swine (Bk. X); and the incident is stock metaphor of Renaissance allegory.
201. *cautility*] cunningness, subtlety.
213. *do for*] act for, attend to.
217. *angels and crowns*] Angels were gold coins (1470–1634); *crowns* were either the gold "crown of the rose" of Henry VIII (1526) or the silver coins of 1551.

Should not our minds rest in full contentation,
Having trust in that treasure most high in respect?
Saint Paul, whom the Lord so high doth erect,
Saith, it passeth the sense, our memories and mind,   225
Much less can our outward eyes the same find.
As for the treasure that you possess here,
Through fickleness of fortune soon fadeth away;
The greatest of renown and most worthy peer,
Sometime in the end falleth to misery and decay.   230
Record of Dionysius a king of much fame,
Of the valiant Alexander, and Caesar the strong
Record of Tarquinus which Superbus had to name,
And of Heliogabalus that minister'd with wrong:
To recite them all it would be very long.   235
But these be sufficient plainly to prove
How soon and uncertainly riches doth remove.

CONTENTATION.

It is true, and therefore a mind well content
Is great riches as wise King Solomon doth say;
For we have seen of late days this canker pestilent   240
Corrupting our realm to our utter decay,
Ambition, I mean, which chiefly doth reign
Amongst those who should have been example to other.
Yea we see how the Brethren they did disdain,

---

224. *Saint Paul*] Perhaps the reference is to II Cor. 4. The notes to Bible,
1551, which are ultimately Tyndale's, identify the god of this world with
Mammon, and in his "Exposition to Math. v, vi, vii" Tyndale calls
Mammon "Covetousness."

230. *Sometime*] at some time in the future.

231–234.] The allusions to those who suffer the fickleness of fortune are
commonplace and may as well come from such medieval compilations as
Lydgate's *Fall of Princes* as from classical sources. Dionysius (l. 231) is
probably the tyrant of Syracuse; Heliogabalus (l. 234) is probably Heliar-
chus, the tyrant of Persia (cf. Bk. IV of *The Fall of Princes*).

233. *which . . . name*] i.e., who was called Tarquinus Superbus (Tarquin
the Proud).

244. *the Brethren*] The term *Brethren* was drawn from the early church and
was used generically for Protestants. Dickens (p. 70) notes that the term
"Christian Brethren" was used in the early Reformation for the secret
society of London merchants engaged in importing English Protestant
books from the continent and that the term was also loosely applied to
Lollards.

And burned with fire the child with the mother.   245
It is often seen that such monstrous ambition,
As spareth not to spill the blood of the innocent,
Will not greatly stick to fall to sedition,
The determinations of God thereby to prevent;
But God I trust shall disappoint their intent,   250
And overthrow the power of fading treasure,
And cause us all to wish for the heavenly pleasure.

HEAVENLY MAN.

O you ancient men whom God hath furnished with fame,
Be ye always mindful to walk in the ways of the just,
And add ever more virtue to your honest name,   255
And at no hand be overcome with covetous or lust,
But in God's holy promise put confidence and trust.
And then double felicity at the last we shall possess,
And then in all earthly doings God shall give good success.
Ye poor men and commons, walk in your vocation,   260
Banish fond fantasies which are not convenient,
Settle your minds with enough to have contentation,
Considering that that leadeth to treasures most excellent;

245.] The reference may be either to the story of Elizabeth Pepper,
burnt at Stratford, who was eleven weeks pregnant (Foxe, *Acts and Monuments* [ed. J. Pratt, London, 1877], VIII, 726), or, as L. B. Wright points
out ("Social Aspects of Some Belated Morality Plays," *Anglia*, LIV [1930],
116), to the story of Perontine Massey who was burnt at Guernsey in 1556.
Foxe included the grisly details. When the ropes holding her to the stake
broke, Perontine, being great with child, fell into the flames; "as the belly
of the woman burst asunder by the vehemency of the flame, the infant,
being a fair man-child fell into the fire, and eftsoons being taken out of the
fire by one W. House, was laid upon the grass. Then was the child had to
the provost, and from him to the bailiff, who gave censure that it should
be carried back again, and cast into the fire, where it was burnt with the
silly mother . . ." (Foxe, *Acts and Monuments*, VIII, 230).
248–252.] These lines reflect the political uncertainty of the opening
years of Elizabeth's reign, and suggest not only Protestant fears but
also their belief in God's providential care for England as his chosen
land.
248. *stick to*] hesitate, scruple.
260. *commons*] those who are neither ennobled nor clerics.
261. *convenient*] morally appropriate, befitting.
263. *that leadeth*] i.e., being satisfied with enough leads to . . . .

For these are uncertain, but they are most parmanent.
Your necessity apply with treasure, faith and trust,   265
And you shall have enough always among the just.

WORLDLY MAN.

And indeed, enough is as good as a feast.
Good Lord, how your words have alter'd my mind;
A new heart methinks is enter'd in my breast,
For no thought of mine old in me I can find.   270
I would to God you would take me in your company,
And learn me how I may be an heavenly man;
For now I perceive this world is but vanity,
Let a man therefore make of it as much as he can.

CONTENTATION.

Do you speak as you think, and as you mind do you say?   275
Could you be content to lead the rules of a godly life?

WORLDLY MAN.

I do mean it truly and I will study them night and day,
For I regard neither treasure, children nor wife.

HEAVENLY MAN.

Give me your hand, then together let us depart.

WORLDLY MAN.

And I will wait on you sir, with all my heart.   280
                                                    Exeunt.

Enter Temerity, Inconsideration *and* Precipitation *singing this song.*

              When Covetous is busy
              Then we three be all merry,
                For he doth trimly invent
              To make us fine frolic cheer,
              Be vitailes never so dear   285
                And all our money clean spent.

280.1. *Exeunt.*]   this   edn.;   *Exeunt*   281–304.] *in* Q *the song, broken a*
Ambo. Q.   *l. 292, is printed in double columns.*

---

264. *these . . . they*] Pronominal reference is often vague or inexact in the
play; *these* refers to worldly treasures, *they* to the heavenly treasures of the
preceding line.

264. *parmanent*] i.e., permanent.

265. *apply*] administer; the word order is inverted and the construction
is imperative.

283. *trimly*] finely.   285. *vitailes*] victuals.

Therefore, we spare for no cost;
We can be trusted of our host
   For shillings twenty and one.
Covetous hath a good wit,   290
He findeth a mean to pay it
   When all our money is gone.
Therefore, troll the bowl to me,
With "huff, childe" and "have to thee,"
   The longest liver pay all.   295
Our trust is in Covetise,
For he is prudent and wise;
   Therefore, money can not fall.
O Covetous, prudent prince,
All strong walls thou dost convince   300
   And rulest them every one;
Thou dost drive many a drift,
And makest for us much shift,
   When all our money is gone.

Enter Covetous *the Vice alone* [*as* Temerity, Inconsideration, *and* Precipitation, *go aside*].

COVETOUS.

At Blackheath field where great Golias was slain,   305

---

293. *troll the bowl*] pass the bowl.
294. *huff*] an exclamation attributed to swaggerers.
294. *have to*] to go at, make an attempt at; here, used colloquially as a challenge in a drinking bout.
300. *convince*] overcome.
302. *drive . . . drift*] instigate many a plot.
303. *makest . . . shift*] make much effort, try all means.
305–352.] These lines are in the medieval tradition of the vaunt of Herod, Pilate, and Satan; cf. the entrance of Wrath in *The Longer*, ll. 636 ff. Wager intermingles local typography, Biblical history, contemporary allusions, fable, and romance. If the result is nonsense which contrasts with the sober reasoning of the preceding section, such mixtures are not uncommon in the period; e.g., Machyn in his diary records that the May Games on June 24, 1559, included Saint John Zacharus, a giant, the nine worthies, Saint George and the dragon, the morris dance, Robin Hood, Little John, Maid Marian, and Friar Tuck (*The Diary of Henry Machyn* [Camden Society, XLII (1848)], p. 201).
305. *Blackheath*] outside London; the field is connected with rebellions of 1496/7 and 1553/4 and was used as a place for jousting.
305. *Golias*] Goliath.

The moon lying in childbed of her last son,
The Tiborne at Warwick was then king of Spain,
By whom the land of Canaan then was won.
It happen'd between Peterborough and Pentecost,
About such time as ivy was made of wormwood.   310
That child's work in Easilwood with fire was lost,
And all through the treason of false Robin Hood,
That saw Sir Guy of Warwick and Colebrand,
Which fought against the sun and stopped his light:
Yea (quoth Hobgoblin) let me take them in hand,   315
Children, children not able to resist my might.
A wonderful bloodshed was in those days,
For Saint Stephen fought against the golden knight:
Insomuch that Peter was fain to give his keys
To those, God knows, that had to them no right.   320
With the grief of that, all the saints in heaven
Proclaimed open wars at Barnard-in-the-Field;
They fought from six of the clock to eleven
Or ever the traitors would give over and yield.
But to say there was triumph, in faith there was;   325
Saint Stephen the younger was made Captain of the Guard.
Wonderful it was to see such things he brought to pass,
As I am sure the like of them ye never heard.
By gis (quoth Saint Stephen) it was time to trudge;
Friar Francis took his flight to Paul's steeple: 330

---

307. *Tiborne*] Tyburn was the place of public execution for Middlesex County and the name may have been used generically for such places.

309. *Peterborough and Pentecost*] the juxtaposition of place and time is comic nonsense.

313. *Sir Guy . . . Colebrand*] Sir Guy fights two Colbrons in the romance: Colbron the Danish giant and Colbron the Champion of the Pagans at the siege of Byzantium (*The History of Guy Earl of Warwick*, Chaps. 8 and 14, in *Early Prose Romances*, ed. W. J. Thoms [London, *n.d.*]).

317–320.] The lines may well refer to events in the reign of Queen Mary: *bloodshed* would refer to the persecutions; *Saint Stephen* might be a romantic allusion to Stephen Gardiner, and Peter's relinquishing of the keys an allusion to the failure of the Catholic cause.

329. *By gis*] oath; "by Jesus."

330–332.] On the fourth of June, 1561, the steeple to St. Paul's was destroyed by fire in a spectacular blaze; but the steeple was often damaged by electrical storms.

In faith he was even with them for an old grudge,
For he carried away the weathercock in spite of the people.
Then was I dubbed knight at Kinistone,
And made officer of all courts and laws;
I gave offices and livings many a one: 335
Marry, indeed you may say it was for a cause.
In faith the same day that midsummer was married,
I never laughed better in my life,
For even suddenly away Saint Uncumber carried
Both the bridegroom and the bride his wife.   340
No remedy on God's name, but I must bear them company.
Cheer, in faith there was, cheer in bowls,
And who was minstrel but Saint Anthony;
He made melody for all Christian souls.
A quarter of a year we tarried there in the tent,   345
Wherein we had capricorn baked like red deer;
I tarried so long till I was shent,
Jesu, how they cried out of me there.
Well, I must abroad among my friends,
Every hour till I come they think a day;   350
I will go among them to fulfill their minds.
Fare ye well, gossip, I must needs away.

[Temerity, Inconsideration, *and* Precipitation *come forward.*]

TEMERITY.

What, brother Covetous? whither away so fast?
I saw you not, by the mass, till I was almost past.

COVETOUS.

What, mine own brother Temerity?   355
I rejoice to see you, I swear by the Trinity.

351. them] *this edn.*; then Q.

---

333. *Kinistone*] Kingston.
339. *Saint Uncumber*] Otherwise known as St. Wilgefortis, St. Uncumber
was a mythical personage. Legend records that she grew a beard and
mustache in order to escape marriage; by tradition she delivers women
from troublesome husbands.
343. *Saint Anthony*] Known as "the Abbot," St. Anthony was the patron
saint of the monastic movement.
346. *capricorn*] goat.   347. *shent*] ruined.
352. *gossip*] i.e., the audience to whom Covetous addresses his vaunt.

INCONSIDERATION.

For thee we three have taken great thought.

PRECIPITATION.

Lord, how far about for you we have sought.

COVETOUS.

And I pray you where have you three sought for me?

PRECIPITATION.

In the King's Bench and in the Marshalsea.   360

Yea, and in all the Counters, and at Newgate,

For these are places meet for thine estate.

COVETOUS.

I perceive well it must be my chance

Above all your kinsfolk you to enhance.

Your place is at Saint Thomas-a-Wat'rings,   365

Or else at Wapping beyond Saint Katherine's.

There will I dub you knights of the halter,

Among your mates there strongly to tolter.

INCONSIDERATION.

You are to blame, in faith, Precipitation,

For you began this fond communication.   370

COVETOUS.

You are knaves to use such salutation.

TEMERITY.

Why, brother, we speak for your consolation.

COVETOUS.

Speak what you will, even with you I can make;

Speak you in mirth, and in mirth I do it take.

But by the mass and if you go about me to flout,   375

368. tolter] *this edn.*; talter *Q*.

360–361. *King's Bench . . . Marshalsea . . . Counters . . . Newgate*] Newgate
was in Faringdon Ward Without; the other three prisons were in Southwark.

362. *meet*] fitting, proper.

364. *enhance*] lift up, elevate.

365. *Saint Thomas-a-Wat'rings*] the location of the gallows for Surrey near
the second milestone on the Kent road.

366. *Wapping . . . Katherine's*] Stow notes that this is "the usual place of
execution for the hanging of Pirats and sea Rovers, at the low water mark
there to remain till three tides had overflowed them" (Stow, II, 70–71).

367. *knights of the halter*] knights of the gallows.

368. *tolter*] turn, toss about.

373. *even . . . make*] to render even; i.e., "I'll be even with you."

I will make the better of all you three a lout.

PRECIPITATION.

No sir, no. We came not hither you to molest;
Our business, I tell you, is very earnest.

INCONSIDERATION.

By God's arse, true. If now we make not shift,
We are all four like to have a great lift.   380

TEMERITY.

If ever Covetous were in danger of punishment,
He standeth now at the point of banishment.

COVETOUS.

Sancti Blaci! you make me much to muse.
Passion of me sirs, why? what news?

PRECIPITATION.

I think the Day of Judgment be now at hand,   385
For it was never thus since the world did stand;
The Worldly Man hath forsaken Covetous clean,
And unto Contentation and Enough he doth lean.

COVETOUS.

What doth he? *Benedicte*, is this true?

INCONSIDERATION.

Yea faith, he is quite becomen anew,   390
Moreover, with the Heavenly Man he is associate,
Where he studieth the rules of godly life early and late.

COVETOUS.

Body of me! Precipitation, fetch me my gown,
My cap, and my chain. I will to the town.

[*Exit* Precipitation.]

Marry, sir, indeed it is time to stir coals;   395
I will go near to fetch some of them out of their holes.

379. arse] *this edn.*; ares Q.

---

379. *By God's arse*] This piquant oath probably derives from Exodus
33:22 where on Mt. Sinai God promises Moses, "Thou shalt see my
back parts but my face thou shalt not see."
380. *to . . . lift*] i.e., to be hanged.
383. *Sancti Blaci*] probably St. Blaise; the blessing of St. Blaise was
invoked against afflictions of the throat, and St. Blaise's Well in Bromley,
Kent, had a local reputation for miraculous cures.
386. *did stand*] existed.
390. *becomen*] to come into existence, perhaps to be reborn.
396. *I . . . near*] "I will be on the point of . . . ."

TEMERITY.

Haste maketh waste, brother Covetous, ye wot;
No love so soon cold as that is most hot.
I warrant you the Worldly Man will soon be weary,
For they will not suffer him once to be merry.   400
And verily he is inclined to be nought;
Therefore, think not that by them he will long be taught.

COVETOUS.

Now by the mass, of one that should have sapience
I never heard none utter such a foolish sentence.
Know you not that whensoever a sinner doth repent   405
That God forgiveth him his wickedness incontinent?

INCONSIDERATION.

True indeed as heretofore hath been seen;
Many have been made heavenly that worldly have been.

[*Enter* Precipitation *with gown, chain, and cap.*]

PRECIPITATION.

Here is your gown, your chain, and your cap.

COVETOUS.

Body of me, but for shame thou shouldst bear me a rap.   410
Whoreson thief, the devil in hell thee choke!
What meanest thou, foolish knave, to bring my cloak?

TEMERITY.

Why, my brother is blind, I hold you a crown;
Body of me, he knoweth not a cloak from a gown.

INCONSIDERATION.

Tush masters, he was stirring in the morning betime;   415
At four of the clock in a cellar he was saying of Prime.

PRECIPITATION.

I blame him not, though betimes he stir,

398.] proverbial; cf. Tilley, L 483: "Hot love is soon cold."
401. *nought*] nothing; but also a pun on "naught," immoral.
406. *incontinent*] immediately.
410. *bear me a rap*] give me a blow.
413. *hold you a crown*] bet you a crown.
416. *Prime*] Prime is the first of the daytime canonical offices; as Precipitation suggests, not only was Covetous up early but he was also befuddled since the appropriate service for this hour would be Lauds, normally sung at dawn.

For he is made aleconner in our parish this year.
His pains is so great in tasting of drink
That many times his eyes into his head do sink,   420
And then he looketh prettily as narrow as a crow;
I tell you he can scarce read the letters of his crossrow.

COVETOUS.

Body of me, you are knaves all three;
Take gown, chain, cap and all for me.
I will be even with you all, I swear by God's mother.   425
Choose you, shift how you can one for another.

Be going out.

I warrant you I shall be able to shift for myself,
Or else you may say I were a foolish elf.

TEMERITY (*hold him*).

Why brother, you said you would all things well take.

COVETOUS.

Yea, but I would not have you your fool me to make,   430

Come in again.

For you know well enough that of you all three
I am worthy the governor and ruler to be.
Covetous (saith the wise man) is the root of all evil;
Therefore, Covetous is the chiefest that cometh from the devil.
But this is that knave I mean, Precipitation;   435
But I will be even with him, I swear by the Passion.

PRECIPITATION.

I am sorry by my truth that you are so sore offended.
What sir, if a fault be made, it shall be amended.

COVETOUS.

Nay faith, I am an aleconner, or some drunken fool!

426.1.] *Q prints to the right of ll. 426–427.*
430.1.] *Q prints to the right of ll. 430–431.*
437.S.P. PRECIPITATION.] *this edn.*; Precipitation. Cum in. *Q.*

---

418. *aleconner*] inspector of ale.
421. *looketh . . . narrow*] Joseph Wright (*The English Dialect Dictionary*, London, 1903) records for Northumberland the phrase "to look narrow" meaning "to wear a somewhat inebriated expression" (IV, 228).
421. *prettily*] passably.
422. *crossrow*] the alphabet, derived from the figure of the cross prefixed to the line of letters.
433. *wise man*] Saint Paul, I Tim. 6:10.

I am no better, but your courage I will cool.   440

He fighteth with them both with his dagger.

That witless knave too, Inconsideration,
He was beginner of this disputation.
But it is no matter; once or Christmas day
I will be even with you, be as be may.
INCONSIDERATION (*lay hold on him*).
    What, worshipful Master Covetous, are you angry with me? 445
    I am sorry for it, man, what can I more be?
    Hang me up by the neck like a strong thief
    If ever I speak any word that shall put you to grief.
COVETOUS.
    I would do for you, sirs, for I love you all three;
    Marry then, I look that, as I am, you should accept me.   450
TEMERITY.
    By my troth brother, I dare say none of us all
    But that to do as you bid us, ready find you shall.
COVETOUS.
    Marry then, on good fellowship let us like friends agree.
ALL.
    Why, above all things that desire we.
COVETOUS.
    Will you help then to make me gay?   455
TEMERITY.
    As you will wish it, so we will you array.
COVETOUS.
    Will you consent to show unto me reverence?
PRECIPITATION.
    Yea, at all times we will show to you our obedience.
COVETOUS.
    Will you take me for your master and head?
INCONSIDERATION.
    Yea marry sir, for so it standeth us in stead.   460

440.1.] *Q prints to the right of ll. 440–*
443.

440.1. *both*] Precipitation and Temerity.
449. *do for*] act for, provide for.
460. *standeth . . . stead*] is to our advantage.

−101−

COVETOUS.

    And do you say as you think in very deed?

TEMERITY.

    Yea, that shall you prove in all time of need.

COVETOUS.

    First, to help on my gown some pains do you take,
    And then I will see what curtsy you can make.

INCONSIDERATION.

    It is trim indeed; by the mass, in that gown   465
    Methinks you be worthy to be mayor of a town.

COVETOUS.

    Say you so? then how like you this countenance?

PRECIPITATION.

    Very comely and like a person of great governance.

COVETOUS.

    Then all is well. Come, come do your duty.

ALL THREE.

    O worthy Prince Covetous, we humbly salute ye.   470

COVETOUS.

    Body of me, that same will mar all
    When in company I come if Covetous you do me call.

TEMERITY.

    Therefore, it is best for us all to change our names.

PRECIPITATION.

    Or else peradventure we shall come to shames.

COVETOUS.

    Well, hold your peace then, let me alone,   475
    And I will devise names for you every one.   *Study* [.]
    Sirrah, nay you gape at me.

TEMERITY.   What shall my name be?

COVETOUS.

    You will have it or I have it, will ye?
    Sirrah, thy name shall be—   *Study.*

PRECIPITATION.   What, I pray you?

COVETOUS.

    A shame take thee, unmannerly lout!   480
    Thou camest so hastily thou hast put me out.

---

467. *countenance*] appearance.

Nay, that maid looks on me.   *Study* [.]

Come hither, Inconsideration, I have a name for thee.

INCONSIDERATION.

Have you sir? I pray you what shall it be?

COVETOUS.

Nay, by the mass, it is gone again.   485

INCONSIDERATION.

And I would know it, I tell you very fain.

COVETOUS.

Yea, but you must tarry till I have it.

TEMERITY [*aside*].

I tell you my brother hath a brave wit.

COVETOUS.

A shame take them, I have them now all three.

Speak to Inconsideration.

Come hither brother, I will tell you what your name shall be, 490

You know that men nowadays to reason do trust,

Therefore, Reason yourself from henceforth name you must.

Temerity, I know well thy quality:

Thou art heady, thou shalt be called Agility.

I study a name for Precipitation if it may hit.   495

Let me see, by my truth, thou shalt be called Ready Wit.

PRECIPITATION.

An excellent name indeed, for I am ready and quick with a pen:

For before I see one, I can condemn ten.

I pass not for any man's matters or cause;

Money and wit shall govern the laws.   500

COVETOUS.

Well, masters, I have chosen names for each one of you,

But mine own name I know not, I make God a vow.

How if I call my name Wit or Policy?

489.1.] *Q prints to the right of ll. 489–*
491.

---

482. *maid*] a girl in the audience; as Craik points out, "the performances of Tudor interludes are meant to draw the adjoining audience into the play" (p. 19).

499. *pass*] care.

503. *Policy*] Around 1550 this term became charged with pejorative meaning derived from its association with Machiavelli and the realities of

TEMERITY.

Marry sir, that agreeth to your nature exceedingly.

COVETOUS.

Truth, for what shall the Worldly Man do with you three,   505
Except to maintain you, he take in me?
Little worth is reason, ready wit, and agility
Except to maintain them there be a policy.
Sirs, you tell me the Worldly Man is converted?

PRECIPITATION.

Yea faith, that forever from us he is departed.   510

COVETOUS.

Forever (quoth he) ha, ha, ha—no, no I warrant thee, I—
What this gear meaneth full well I do espy.
Tush, he purposeth to go both to heaven and to hell
And fetch news from thence to the people to tell;
He will be a prophet that was wont to be a devil.   515

TEMERITY.

But his prophecy, I think, will prove but evil.

INCONSIDERATION.

Well, no more words, enough is as good as a feast;
They say it is perilous with edge-tools to jest.

COVETOUS.

Now sirs, I will tell you, this is all my drift,
To get the Worldly Man hither by some shift.   520
Temerity, thou shalt with him thyself acquaint
And what thou canst do, to him forth thou shalt paint.
Virtue is made an error by Temerity,
For stoutly he standeth against the verity;
For temerity learned men do say   525
Is a quality to do all things without delay.
So that if thou mayest get into his habitation,
He will soon be weary of Enough and Contentation.
Then with him shall work Precipitation,

514. fetch] *this edn.*; feth *Q*.

practical politics. "Policy" tends to be substituted for "gear" in the vocabulary of the Vice as his trickery is redefined (B. Spivak, *Shakespeare and the Allegory of Evil* [New York, 1958], 373–376).

518. *edge-tools*] any instrument with a sharp cutting edge: a knife or a sword.

523.] i.e., "fools rush in where angels fear to tread."

Who is of this property and inclination   530
To see and to do all without forecast,
Not thinking of things to come or of things past.
Therefore, after that Temerity doth once enter,
Thou shalt put thy service in adventer.
Then Inconsideration shall get into his mind   535
Who is a quality much of the same kind.
He weigheth neither the time, person, nor place,
Neither (as they say) the tail nor the face;
Thus if you three within him once be placed,
You shall see that Enough of him shall soon be disgraced.   540
Under the name of Policy to enter I do not doubt,
And I being enter'd Enough shall be cast out,
For where Covetous in any place doth remain,
There Content with Enough cannot abide certain.
So that he shall run hedling into the pit,   545
Doing all things hedling without modesty or wit.
Lo here to you my mind I have disclosed,
All have I said that I have now purposed.

TEMERITY.

By the faith of my body, it is worthily devised.

COVETOUS.

In all thy haste go thou and be thou disguised.   550
Marry now, there cometh another thing to my remembrance;
Are none of you acquainted with ghostly Ignorance?

INCONSIDERATION.

What he? pardy, he is my ghostly father.

COVETOUS.

I would speak with him so much the rather,
For divers causes that I do consider.   555
My brother and thou shall depart hence together.
Look you make you trim as fast as you can,

538. the face] *this edn.*; the the face   550. thy] *this edn.*; the Q.
Q.

---

534. *put . . . in adventer*] hazard your services.
545. *hedling*] headlong.
553. *pardy*] by God; a mild oath which often meant no more than "verily."
553. *ghostly father*] spiritual father; i.e., priest.
554. *the rather*] the more.

And then in haste seek to speak with the Worldly Man.
Inconsideration to ghostly Ignorance, thou shalt resort,
And this message from me to him thou shalt report.   560
First, that he name himself Devotion
And we will help him to dignity and promotion.
Charge him not to be out of the way
For we purpose to send for him this present day.

TEMERITY.

For as much as you put your trust and confidence in me,   565
What I can do for you, or it be long, you shall see.

INCONSIDERATION.

Where to find ghostly Ignorance I am sure,
Seldom or never at home at his own cure.

PRECIPITATION.

No, the sermons that ghostly Ignorance hath made
Hath almost brought all the parishes in England out of trade. 570

COVETOUS.

Well, hie you a pace, that you were gone.
Precipitation and I will tarry here alone.

TEMERITY.

Farewell, Covetous, till we meet again.

INCONSIDERATION.

That shall not be long if our purpose we obtain.

COVETOUS.

Nay hear you? God be with you, will you be gone?   575
Body of me, you are no better than knaves every one.
Farewell Covetous? nay, farewell good lob!
                              [Temerity *and* Inconsideration] *be going out.*
You have even as much manners as hath a dog.
                              [Temerity *and* Inconsideration] *come in.*
Plain Covetous? this is according to promise is it not?
Well, what I intend to do for it, I wot what I wot.   580

564. purpose] *this edn.*; porpose *Q*.   578.1.] *Q prints to the right of l. 578.*
577.1.] *Q prints to the right of l. 577.*

568. cure] parish.
569–570.] One of the principal concerns of the Reformation was to
provide adequate preachers for parish churches; here the allusion is to the
quality of Ignorance's sermons (or ironically, to their infrequency) which
has deprived (*brought . . . out of*) the parish of its trade.
577. lob] country bumpkin, clown.   580. wot] know.

TEMERITY.

    I cry you mercy, right worshipful Master Covetise,

    Most prudent, politic, sapient and wise.

INCONSIDERATION.

    Pardon us by my truth, it was but forgotten.

COVETOUS.

    Nay, I take it even thus, soon ripe, soon rotten.

    I am nobody with you, but by Him I swear   585

    I look the greatest stroke amongst you to bear.

TEMERITY.

    Enough is as good as a feast; we are warned I trow,

    From henceforth our duties I warrant ye we will show,

    We take our leave of you, noble prince Covetise,

    The king, emperor, yea the god of all vice.   590

INCONSIDERATION.

    O worthy visage, and body well compact,

    O goodly man in wit, work and fact,

    We simple creatures do show to you obedience,

    Being minded to depart under your patience.

COVETOUS.

    Yea marry, this is somewhat like the matter.   595

PRECIPITATION [aside].

    Crafty knaves, how they can a fool flatter.

COVETOUS.

    Fare ye well both, give me your hands one after another.

    I love ye as dearly as the children of my mother.

                              Exeunt ambo.

    How say'st thou, Precipitation? How likest thou this matter?

PRECIPITATION.

    By my truth, I will tell the truth, yea and not flatter.   600

    I perceive well enough what herein you do mean.

    You will not leave till you have marred him clean,

    Not only riches singular and private,

    But also public weal's you will spoliate.

598.1.] *after l. 596 in* Q.

---

581. *Covetise*] The normal substantive form is used here for its pretentiousness.

586. *stroke*] authority, influence.

603. *singular*] individual.

For I perceive by your former monition   605
That through ghostly Ignorance you will destroy devotion,
I mean true faith in God's love and hope,
And cause him in clear sunshine for light to grope.

COVETOUS.

Thou thinkest as truth is in very deed;
I intend no less if my device may likely speed.   610
There will I begin and if error once rage in religion,
I warrant thee in public weal will soon be division.

PRECIPITATION.

Well, what you intend to me doth not appertain;
My nature is to rage where haste doth reign.
And what causeth haste? but only Temerity   615
That maketh fools hardy with security.
Precipitation forth doth this Worldly Man lead
So that all his affairs be done rudely on head;
Then Inconsideration both night and day
Shall prompt him forward nothing at all to weigh,   620
Neither to consider his beginning,
Neither at the end what shall be the winning.
So that if all we do our proper nature and kind,
He shall not regard who shall the profit find.

COVETOUS.

Lupus est in fabula, no more words.   625

PRECIPITATION.

I never fear any such kind of bourds.
This is the Worldly Man, I suppose indeed.

Enter the Worldly Man *and* Enough. *Let the* Worldly Man *stand afar off in a strange attire* [*with* Enough].

COVETOUS.

To work wisely with him I see we had need.

WORLDLY MAN.

I find it true as the wise king Solomon doth say,

620. prompt] *this edn.*; promp *Q*.

---

605. *monition*] warning.
625. *Lupus . . . fabula*] Tilley, W 607, "Speak of the wolf and he will appear"; cf. Erasmus, *Adagia*, 916A which T. Elyot cites in *The Dictionary of Syr Thomas Elyot* (1538).
626. *bourds*] idle tales, jests.   629. *Solomon*] Prov. 15:16.

ENOUGH IS AS GOOD AS A FEAST

It is better to have a little with the fear of the Lord   630
Than to have much treasure and yet go astray,
I mean to decline from God's holy word.
The proverb saith enough is as good as a feast;
He that hath enough and cannot be content
In my judgment is worse than a beast,   635
For he wanteth a good conscience, mind and intent.

ENOUGH (*poorly arrayed*).

The chariot of Covetous, as Bernard doth write,
On four wheels of vices is carried away;
And these be the four vices that he doth recite:
Contempt-of-God, Forgetfulness-of-death-each-day,   640
Faint-courage, and Ungentleness he doth say.
These be the wheels that to adversity's cart doth belong;
These have persuasions to beguile men many and strong.
The same chariot hath two horses which doth it draw;
The one named Raveny and the other Nigardship;   645
Their carter is Desire-to-have, who always doth claw,
By fraud or guile one another to nip.
This carter hath two cords to his whip,
The one is Appetite and Felicity-for-to-get,
The other is called Dread and Fear-to-forlet.   650

WORLDLY MAN.

When this chariot goes in the ground of man's mind,
He is not once able to think a good thought,
For Covetous doth the heart so much to lucre bind
That he judgeth all things to be vain and nought
Except some gain or profit thereby be brought.   655
I myself am able to say it, for I do it know;
To have gotten money I studied to deceive high and low.

637.S.P. ENOUGH (*poorly arrayed*).]   649. Appetite] *this edn.*; Appititite
this edn. Poorly arayed Inough. Q.   Q.
643. have] *this edn.*; bave Q.

---

637. *Bernard*] Bernard of Clairvaux; the relevant passage occurs in *A Monomachie of Motives* (trans. A. Fleming, 1582), "The xv Combat" (pp. 161–162), which was attributed to Bernard.
645. *Raveny*] robbery, rapine.   646. *carter*] driver.
646. *claw*] flatter, fawn as well as scratch.
650. *Fear-to-forlet*] abandon fear.
651. *ground*] bottom, lowest part.

–109–

But thanks be to God the father of all might,
Which will not the death of sinners as Scripture doth say,
It hath pleased him to open unto me the true light   660
Whereby I perceive the right path from the broad way;
Therefore, I am content myself for to stay
With Enough which bringeth me to quiet in body and mind;
Yea, and all other commodities therewith I do find.

ENOUGH.

Godliness is great riches if a man can be content   665
When God hath sent him plenty and enough;
Let us praise him for our food and raiment,
And live godlily all our lives through;
For we must tread the paths of death so sharp and rough.
And then shall we be sure to carry as little away   670
As we brought with us, thus Saint Paul doth say.

COVETOUS.

Body of me, he is marvelous foregone;
We shall have somewhat to do with him anon.

PRECIPITATION.

It was ill luck that he came not alone.
I would that beggarly knave in hell were.   675

COVETOUS.

Well, let me alone; I will go near
To cause him of his company to be weary.
I have done as great acts thrice this year;
I am not to learn to row in Illiran's ferry.

660. the] *this edn.*; the the *Q*.

658–659. *God . . . sinners*] The wording here is that of the opening sentence of the Absolution in the service of Morning Prayer (first introduced
in the 1552 Prayer Book); the scriptural reference might be to Ezekiel
18:32: " . . . I have no pleasure in the death of him that dyeth, sayeth the
Lorde GOD" (Bible, 1551) or Ezekiel 33:11: " . . . I have no pleasure in
the deathe of the wycked" (Bible, 1551).

661. *broad way*] The language here echoes Math. 7:13–14.

665–671.] I Tim. 6:6–8: "Godliness is greate ryches, if a man be content with that he hath. For we brought nothyng into the worlde, and it is
a playne case that we can carye nothynge out. When we have foode and
rayment, let us therewith be content" (Bible, 1551).

679. *Illiran's ferry*] If this is not an allusion to a contemporary ferry,
Illiran's may be a mistake for "Charon's." The line would be Covetous'
boast that he is not about to die in defeat.

I will go to him and thou shalt wait upon me;   680
Thou shalt hear what a tale to him I will tell.

PRECIPITATION.

If thou speed well now, I dare promise thee
The devil will give thee the crown of hell.

[Enough *comes forward.*]

COVETOUS.

God speed you sir, I pray you, might I be so bold
As to have a word or two with you in your ear?   685

ENOUGH.

Yea, hardily my friend, say what you would.
Your mind unto me you may boldly declare.

COVETOUS.

I pray you, are you not acquainted with this gentleman?
I would fain speak with him a word or twain alone;
I beseech you help me to my request if you can,   690
For I have haste on my way, I must needs be gone.

ENOUGH.

If you had required a greater thing of me,
I would have done it for you I tell you certain.

[*Goes to* Worldly Man.]

Sir, one of yonder men which you do see
Would speak with you alone very fain.   695

WORLDLY MAN.

I will go to him and know his mind.—
Is it you that would speak with me, my friend?

COVETOUS.

Yea, forsooth sir.

WORLDLY MAN.   What say you to me?

COVETOUS.

O sir, O good sir, O, O, O, my heart will break—
O, O, for sorrow God wot, I cannot speak.   *Weep.*   700

WORLDLY MAN.

What is the matter? wherefore weep you thus?

[Covetous] *weep.*

701.1.] *Q prints weep to the right of   participate in the ruse.*
702.S.P., *but Precipitation does not*

686. *hardily*] certainly, freely.

PRECIPITATION.

    Pure love causeth him sir, iwus.

    I am sure that he loves you at the heart.

WORLDLY MAN.

    I thank him truly, it is undeserved on my part.—

    Gentle friend, I pray you cease your lamentation;   705

    Sure it is a strange thing to see a man weep on this fashion.

Let the Vice *weep and howl and make great lamentation to the* Worldly Man.

COVETOUS.

    I cannot choose, O, O, I cannot choose.

    Whow! I cannot choose if my life I should lose.

    To hear that I hear—O, well, it is no matter.

    O, O, O, I am not he that any man will flatter.   710

WORLDLY MAN.

    To hear what you hear? Why, what hear you of me?

PRECIPITATION.

    Marry sir, he heareth that wonderfully changed you be.

WORLDLY MAN.

    I am so indeed, for that I give God the glory;

    And if you be my friend, for my change you are not sorry.

    I trust I have chosen all for the best,   715

    For my former wickedness I hate and detest.

COVETOUS.

    Whow! nay, I would to God that were the worst,

    But I shall have ill will, I think I am accurst.

WORLDLY MAN.

    I judge him not to be of a discreet mind

    That for the truth will be angry with his friend.   720

    The talk of talkers' tongues I do not much weigh;

    Yet I pray you heartily tell me what they say.

COVETOUS.

    Covetous, covetous, every man saith you be.

    A shame take them all prattling knaves for me;

    I am of such a nature as no man is but I,   725

703. he] *this edn.*; be *Q*.   *707–710.*
706.1.] *Q prints to the right of ll.*

702. *iwus*] variant form of iwis.
725–726.] Covetous contrasts his extreme sensitivity (*as no man is but I*) to the insensitivity of prattling knaves. He is so sensitive that he had rather die than hear his friend maligned.

To hear my friend ill-spoken of I had rather die.
Yea wisse man, you are called even so,
All the country of you speak both shame and woe.
He was wont (saith one) to keep a good house,
But now (saith another) there is no living for a mouse.   730
WORLDLY MAN.

If this be the worst, for their talk I do not care;
Let them say so still hardily and do not spare.
I trust I have chosen with Mary the better part.
PRECIPITATION.

O, yet good sir, this grieveth him to the heart.
COVETOUS.

Yea God wot, it is none other, it is none other.   735
I love you as well as mine own born brother.
Think you that it grieveth me not to hear each boy and girl
To say that the Worldly Man is become a churl?
WORLDLY MAN.

He had need to live very circumspectly
That would take upon him to please all men directly.   740
Behold Enough.   *Go towards him.*
COVETOUS (*pluck him back*).

Nay hear you, this grieveth me worst, so God me save.
They say you keep company with every beggarly knave.
WORLDLY MAN.

Where I keep company they have nought to do;
As near as I can, into none but honest company I go.   745
See you, I pray you, Enough.
COVETOUS.

Nay but hear you, is Enough his name?
WORLDLY MAN.

Yea indeed, it is even the very self same.

742.S.D. *pluck him back*] Q *prints to*   748. is] *this edn.*; ls Q.
the right of ll. 742–743.

727. *wisse*] know; the verb form here is difficult to explain since *wisse*
would normally be past tense, but in Scots it is at times used for present
tense.

733. *Mary*] Luke 10:38–42. In interpreting this passage, the Reformation
denied the medieval contrast between the Active and Contemplative lives
symbolized by the two sisters; Martha is excessive and is "troubled about
many thynges" whereas Mary has "chosen the hearing of the word of
God" (Bible, 1551). Cf. Calvin's discussion in *Commentary on a Harmony of
the Evangelists* (Grand Rapids, Mich., 1957), II, 141–145.

COVETOUS.

Saint Dunstan! a man would not judge it by his coat.
Now truly I would not take him to be worth a groat.   750
Hark you, hark you, in faith know you not me?

WORLDLY MAN.

No truly, that I wot of I did you never see.

PRECIPITATION.

That is marvel indeed the truth for to tell;
I dare say your father knew us both very well.

COVETOUS.

Did you never hear him speak of one Policy?   755

WORLDLY MAN.

Yes, that I have, sure an hundred times verily.

COVETOUS.

I am he verily and this your friend Ready Wit,
With whom to be acquainted for you it is fit.

PRECIPITATION.

Truth indeed as Seneca sayeth wittily:
The wise man and not the rich is void of misery.   760

WORLDLY MAN.

Policy and Ready Wit: now the truth is so,
There is no man living that can spare you two.
I trust God worketh for me happily indeed
To send me all such things whereof I have need.
For without a ready wit, who can answer make?   765
Without a policy all commodities will slake.
A ready wit will soon gather and conceive
What he shall forsake and what he shall receive.
Truly now I remember a saying of Tully the divine,
Where he doth both wisdom and learning define.   770
Learning maketh young men sober (saith he)
And it causeth old men of good comfort to be.
Policy is the riches and possession of the poor,

760. is] *this edn.*; ls *Q*.   769. Truly] *this edn.*; Teuely *Q*.

749. *Saint Dunstan*] In the tenth century, St. Dunstan was the chief adviser to King Eldred. His feast day was remembered in the dioceses of Westminster, Birmingham, Clifton, and Southwark; two London churches were dedicated to him.

Yea it garnisheth the rich with goodly adore,
So that there is no strait calling or degree   775
That may conveniently without you be.
Give me your hands for you are welcome heartily.
I am exceeding joyful of your good company.
Enough, I beseech you, bid my friends welcome hither,
For from henceforth we must dwell all together.   780

ENOUGH.

Be not rash in taking of a friend, Aristotle doth say;
Nor when thou hast taken him, cast him not away.
Admit not thy friend either high or low,
Except his behavior to others thou dost know.
For look how before he hath served his other friend,   785
Even so will he serve thee also in the end.

WORLDLY MAN.

Your parables truly I do not well understand.
Except you mean I should have no friend but you by me to stand.

ENOUGH.

Enough is as good as a feast, well you wot,
More than enough, a man needeth not;   790
Whether it be lands, money, friends or store,
If he have enough, what needeth he any more?

COVETOUS.

I perceive that against us two you do grutch.
Can a man of policy and ready wit have too much?
The noble King Solomon was rich and had wisdom great
    store.   795
Yet he ceased not daily to pray to God for more.

PRECIPITATION.

Get thee store of friends (saith Cicero) for it is deemed,
A true friend more than kinsfolk is to be esteemed.

ENOUGH.

It is an old proverb and of an ancient time
Which saith, it is not all gold that like gold doth shine.   800
No more are all friends that friendship pretend,

---

774. *adore*] apparently Wager's coinage for the sake of rhyme; the
meaning is clearly "adornment."
793. *grutch*] complain.

As is approved with many in the end.

WORLDLY MAN.

Yea Enough, but I am sure that this Policy
And this Ready Wit are my friends verily.

COVETOUS.

Are we? yea, faith thereof you may be sure   805
We are they which your wealth shall procure;
Enough is not enough without us two,
For having not us, what can Enough do?
Enough is maintained by wisdom and policy
Which is contained of a ready wit naturally.   810

PRECIPITATION.

Having a ready wit and of policy the skill,
You need not to care for this Enough except you will.
There is another Enough which is invisible,
Which Enough, to want is impossible.
As for this, Enough is enough I cannot deny,   815
But this Enough serveth but even competently.
You have no more now than doth yourself serve,
So that your poor brethren for all you may starve;
But enough that cometh by us twain
Is able yourself and many other to sustain.   820

WORLDLY MAN.

Your words are even as true as the Gospel,
As one named Reason of late to me did tell;
You may be more heavenly, saith he, having riches
Than if you had nothing, the truth to express.
And I find his words true, for when alms I would give,   825
I have not wherewith the needy to relieve.
Enough I have for myself I cannot say nay,
But I would I had more to succor the needy alway.

ENOUGH.

These words proceed from a covetous mind

802. is] *this edn.*; it *Q*.   805. yea] *this edn.*; ye *Q*.

811–820.] The distinction which Precipitation makes between the two
Enough's is obscured by the complexity of the syntax. In ll. 813–814
invisible means "not in sight," i.e., "not present" on stage; and the construction seems to be elliptic, i.e., "with this enough, it is impossible to
want." In l. 816 *competently* means "sufficient, but not going beyond this."
824. *truth to express*] i.e., "to tell the truth."

And from a worldly lust which doth you blind.   830
Was not that poor widow for her offering praised more
Than all they that offer'd of their superfluity and store?
The sacrifice of God as the prophet David doth say
Is a broken heart and a good mind alway.

COVETOUS.

He says well, by Lady, yea and like an honest man,   835
But yet sir, riches to be good, well prove I can.
For every man is not called after one sort,
But some are called to prophesy, some to preach and exhort,
And he, by that means, heaven joys to win.
But every man knoweth not that way to walk in;   840
Therefore, every man (as his vocation is) must walk.
I am sure that against this you will not talk.

ENOUGH.

The greatest boasters are not the best givers,
Nor the earnest preachers are the best livers;
As lucre increaseth riches and honor,   845
So covetous enlargeth daily more and more.
I know some in this realm which once were content
With poorly enough which God to them had sent,
Wishing of a good conscience, as they said verily,
That God would once again restore the verity.   850
If it please thee, good Lord (said they) thy word to us again send
And then truly our covetous lives we will amend.
But since it hath pleased God, them to wealth to restore,
They are ten times more covetous than they were before.
Yea hedling without all consideration   855

831–832.] Luke 21:1–4; cf. v. 4: "For they all haue of their super-
fluytye added unto the offerynge of God: but she, of her penury, hath cast
in al the substance that she had" (Bible, 1551).

833. *David*] Psalm 51:17.

838.] cf. Romans 12:6–8.

841. *vocation*] calling, used in the theological sense of the particular
function or station to which a person is called by God.

847–852.] The allusion here is to the covetousness of the Reformers
during the reign of Edward VI and to their desire during Mary's reign for
the return of the Reformation (*the verity*); cf. Dickens, pp. 205–217, 254–258.

855–860.] Wager alludes here not only to the general economic dis-
locations of the period but also to the acute problem of church income.
Parliament in 1559 passed a bill authorizing the Queen to exchange

They for covetous make some laws in that nation;
Such buying and selling of leases and benefices,
Such doubling of wares to extreme prices,
So shamefully God's ministers they poll and shave
That not half enough to live upon they have.   860
But it is an old saying and a true certainly:
It will not out of the flesh that is bred in the bone verily.
The worldly man will needs be a worldly man still.
Well, choose you; I will let you alone, do what you will.
I cannot think but those that of me hold scorn   865
Will be glad of me or ever the year be half worn.   *Exit.*

WORLDLY MAN.

Marry, farewell! adieu to the devil.
Body of me, he would make me his drivel.

COVETOUS.

You may see what a trusty friend he is.

WORLDLY MAN.

A beggarly knave, I warrant you by the bliss.   870
And even so he and they went about me to make;
Within a while I should have gone to the hedge for a stake.

PRECIPITATION.

I warrant you that you should have proved shortly;
They would not have left you one groat nor penny.
I marvel you would tarry with them any time or season,   875
You are old enough, I trow, to be ruled by reason.

WORLDLY MAN.

A shame take them all, I have spent on them twenty pound
That I had of money and of mine own good ground.

Bishops' lands for "parsonages impropriate and tenths" by which the church's economic position was seriously weakened; cf. J. Strype, *Annals of the Reformation* (Oxford, 1820), VII, 142 ff., and C. Hill, *Economic Problems of the Church from Archbishop Whitgift to the Long Parliament* (Oxford, 1956), Chaps. 1 and 2.

859. *poll*] plunder.   859. *shave*] fleece, extort.

862.] i.e., innate character cannot be eradicated; Tilley, F 365.

868. *drivel*] drudge, fool.

870. *by the bliss*] i.e., by heaven; *the bliss* is the perfect joy of heaven, hence the place of bliss.

871. *to make*] to cause to become; i.e., they sought to make me a beggarly knave.

872. *gone . . . stake*] been reduced to beggary.

I am ashamed of myself, so God me save,
Because I have sold almost all that ever I have.   880
My friends and companions when I go in the street,
So God help me, I am ashamed with them to meet.

COVETOUS.

Passion of me, it was time to look about,
They would quite have undone you or else without doubt.
But I trow, I trow, if you will be ruled by me,   885
What I will do for you, or ere it be long you shall see.
A thousand, thousand, thousand ways I can invent
To fetch in double as much as you have spent.

WORLDLY MAN.

Be ruled by you? Yes, here I do you both embrace
As mine own mind to follow all my life's space.   890
For I tell you plain, I am weary of their school.

PRECIPITATION.

It is time for you, else they would have made you a fool.

WORLDLY MAN.

I perceived no less indeed by the talk of Reason,
But so it should have come to pass in season.

COVETOUS.

And do you my brother Reason perfectly know?   895

WORLDLY MAN.

Yea, and with him one called Agility, I trow.
Reason came to me, and *mihi flectere mentem*, he said,
Sola solet ratio, dux fida sophorum est—it cannot be denied.
To nature and reason he doth open injury
Which of other men counsel doth seek.   900
God hath given men reason and their wits policy,
To forsake that is ill and to take that he doth like.

PRECIPITATION.

And believe you not these words to be very true?

898. *sophorum*] *this edn.*; sophorn *Q.*

880.] Craik (p. 106) notes the irony here between Christ's command to
the rich young man to sell all that he hath and Worldly Man's shame; cf.
Mark 10.
884. *else*] otherwise. Note the inverted word order: *or else* belongs at the
beginning of the line.
897–898. *mihi . . . est*] "he said, 'Reason alone is accustomed to direct
my mind; it is the true leader of the wise.'"

WORLDLY MAN.

Yea, and I have thought on them twenty times since I tell you.
O sirs, methinks if I had money and treasure again,   905
In faith I would be a lively lad, I tell you plain.
Heavenly Man (quoth he) let them be heavenly for me;
The best heaven methinks is rich for to be.

COVETOUS.

In faith it shall cost me and my friends a fall
But you shall be twice as rich as you were before.   910
We will do it to spite them, even with all,
Though we do hundreds wrong therefore.
I have set some aloft in a high place
Which had rather die, I dare well say,
Than one inch of their state should fall or abase,   915
But rather to climb up higher if they may.
Whow! of this world I rule the whole state.
Yea faith, I govern all laws, rites and orders;
I, at my pleasure, raise war, strife and debate,
And again I make peace in all coasts and borders.   920
Nay, yet a much more marvel than that,
Behold, see you this little pretty hand?
This is an arm of steel, for it overthroweth flat
The strongest walls and towers in a whole land.
Power I have laws to alter and make,   925
And all laws made are guided by me;
All that is done is done wholly for my sake,
What strength I have by this you may see.
Moreover, I have in this little hand
The hearts of all men and women upon earth;   930
I rule them both by sea and by land;
Plenty I make and I make also dearth.
Whow, it is wonderful that is done by policy.
While you live take heed; strive not against policy.
The best of them all are glad of policy,   935
Yea in Westminster Hall they use much policy.

908. heaven methinks is] *this edn.*;
heauen is me thinks is *Q*.

911. *even*] square accounts.
915. *abase*] be lowered, humbled.

WORLDLY MAN.

Prudentia noscit omnia, saith the noble man Tully;
Policy knoweth all things both good and ill truly.
O Policy, what meant I from Reason and thee to stray?
Never will I forsake you nor yours after this day.   940
O help me Policy, help me to some money
Whose taste I love better than the taste of honey.

PRECIPITATION.

Sith worthy Policy you have entertained,
Now none of his instruments must be disdained.

WORLDLY MAN.

Disdained? No faith, let him teach me what he will,   945
And I will do it if it were mine own father to kill.

COVETOUS.

Say you so? By the mass, give me your hand.
Come, go with me; let us no longer idle stand.

Go out all three together and make you ready straight ways. Enter Heavenly
Man.

HEAVENLY MAN.

O how hard a thing and difficult it is
For them that in their riches do trust   950
To enter into the kingdom of heaven or bliss.
The words of our Savior to be true grant we must,
It is as easy for a camel through an needle's eye to thrust
As for him that on riches hath fixt his mind
The way to eternal salvation to find.   955
Example hereof you see with your eyes
Of the Worldly Man given to vain pleasure.

---

937. *noscit*] *this edn.*; nosct *Q*.   948.1. *Go . . . ways.*] *Q prints to the*
946. mine] *this edn.*; mine *Q*.   *right of ll. 948–951.*

---

937. *Prudentia . . . omnia*] "prudence knows all."
943. *Sith*] since.
948.1. *you*] Precipitation, who will appear as Tenant (Craik, p. 33).
949–955] Wager may be conflating two passages of Scripture: Math.
19:24 ff.: "Verely I say unto you: it is hard for a ryche man to enter into
the kingdome of heauen . . ." and Luke 18:25 ff.: "with what difficulte
shall they that have ryches enter into the kingdome of God: it is easyer
for a camell to go thorow a nedles eye then for a ryche man to enter the
kingdome of God" (Bible, 1551).

He promised, you heard, from sin to arise
And said he would not love neither money nor treasure
But as he ought to love it, that is in a due measure.   960
But behold how quickly his promise he hath broke,
Whereby he kindleth God's wrath against him to smoke.
For now hath he entertained to him Temerity,
Precipitation and heady Inconsideration;
These cause him to work all things headily,   965
And covet to be had in reputation.
Then Covetous disguiseth himself on such a fashion
That as Seneca saith, he doth good to no man,
But hurt, and most to himself as time shall prove when.   *Exit.*

Enter an old man Tenant *and speak Cotswold speech.*

TENANT.

Alaz, alaz, to whom should I make my moan?   970
Forever and a day cham quite undone.
My landlord is zo covetous as the devil of hell;
Except chill give him such a shameful rent,
As cham not able, away ich must incontinent.
Chave dwelt there this zix and thirty year,   975
Yea these vorty, ich may tell you well near,
And ich never paid above yearly vive pound:
And by our Lady, that to be enough chave vound.
Well, now I must give him even as much more,
Or else ich must void the next quarter or bevore.   980
O masters, is not this even a lamentable thing,
To zee how landlords their poor tenants do wring?
And they are not zo covetous to ask nother, ich believe,
But a zort of vools are as ready to give,

969.1.] *Q prints to the right of ll. 970–*   981. thing] *this edn.*; dhing *Q.*
972.

966. *covet*] The verb here is used as a substantive.
969.1. *Cotswold*] Wager uses the old dramatic tradition of Gloucester-
shire dialect for comic rusticity. In the dialect initial "f" and "s" become
"v" and "z" and the dialectal forms *ich, cham, chill, chave* (I, I am, I will,
I have) are used, although Wager is not consistent.
970. *moan*] lament.
983. *nother*] dialectal form of "another."

And especially strangers—yea a shameful zorte,   985
Are placed now in England and that in every port—
That we, our wives and children, no houses can get
Wherein we may live, such price on them is zet.
Chad thought awhile ago my landlord would not have done
    thus,
For he said he would be a heavenly man iwus;   990
But zoul, the devil is as heavenly as he:
Three times worse than he was bevore as var as I can zee.

Enter poorly [dressed] Servant.

SERVANT.

Body of me, this would make a man to swear!
A shame take them, marry, that ever they came there.
Nay by gisse, I thought he would not be heavenly long,   995
For that to his nature were clean contrary and wrong.
Yonder are such a sort of rutterkins lively and jolly
That all that can be gotten is little enough for their belly.
Soul! we work, we labor, and that night and day,
Yet can we scant have meat and drink the truth to say.   1000
And that which we have is ill enough for dogs,
And we are served withal like a many of hogs.

TENANT.

What, servant? I pray thee what news with thee?

SERVANT.

By my truth, Father Tenant, even as you see.

985. yea] *this edn.*; ye *Q*.   *edn.*; poorly Seruant *Q*.
992.1. *poorly [dressed]* Servant] *this*

---

985. *strangers*] The immigration of Flemish weavers goes back to the
fourteenth century, but the problem was intensified by the flood of immigrants during the Reformation. During Edward's reign, there were some
5,000 fugitives from the religious persecutions in France and the Nether-
lands in London alone (Dickens, pp. 235–236). During the first decade of
her reign, Elizabeth encouraged immigration as part of her maneuvering
against Spain; by 1563 there were some 18,000–20,000 immigrants in the
London and Sandwich areas, by 1566 some 30,000 (Black, *Reign of Elizabeth*
[Oxford, 1936], p. 89).
    997. *rutterkins*] bullies.
    1000. *scant*] scarcely.
    1002. *many*] herd; as a substantive, *many* is apparently confused with
"meinie."

Kept like no man's servant, but rather like a slave,   1005
That I am weary of my life, I tell you, so God me save.
My master taketh on like the devil of hell;
There was never one so hasty, cruel and fell.
But so covetous—Lord! Lord!—you will not believe.
I think all his mind and study to bribery he doth give.   1010

Enter Hireling.

HIRELING.

Now a pestilence take him, vile canker'd churl!
He is neither good to man, women, boy nor girl.
Is this the heavenly man? a shame take him else.
Body of me, in all wickedness he now excels.
And if a thing come in his head, be it good or ill,   1015
Without all wit or reason do it he will.
But so covetous, Lord! I think if he might choose
The dropping of his nose he would not lose.
Every week truly, nay then every day,
He must have account how many eggs his hens lay.   1020
Why, there was never seen such a miser as he,
That the plague cut the throat of him for me.
I have wrought for him this half year by the week,
And now my work is done my money is to seek.
If I and all mine should starve for money,   1025
Of him I dare say I should not get one penny.
A shame take him! how well the Scripture of him is weighed
Which saith, sleep not till the hireling thou hast paid.

TENANT.

I see well that I complain not of him alone,
But others, as well as I, have good cause to moan.   1030
Well, Servant, weeping will not help this gear;
But God will plague him for it, I do not fear.

SERVANT.

I told you, Hireling, how you should be served.

HIRELING.

What, Servant, thou lookest as though thou were starved.

1008. *fell*] fierce, cruel.
1011. *canker'd*] malignant, corrupt.
1027. *Scripture*] Deut. 24:15.

TENANT.

He looketh as lustily, freshly and as well   1035
As all the servants that with his master do dwell.

HIRELING.

His master? why, he is no better than a thief,
For so that he may have it, he cares not who suffer grief.

TENANT.

Nay, by the mass, that words is but too true;
So that his riches increaseth, he careth not who rue.   1040

SERVANT.

I know the occasion of all this gear,
But I would not for twenty pound it should come to his ear.
He saith that he will never leave his extortion
Till of riches he hath gotten an innumerable portion.
He will build, plant, set and sow   1045
Till such a fame of him abroad there grow
That there is none like to him in all the country,
And so by that means he shall come to authority.

HIRELING.

But lightly those that come to authority after that rate
Do end their lives in some miserable and unhappy state.   1050

TENANT.

Thou fool (saith Christ) this night will I fetch thy soul from thee,
And then who shall have the things that thine be?
Well, let him alone, I hope all will prove for the best;
Even as he leadeth his life so shall he find rest.

SERVANT.

Peace, peace, for God's sake, look where the Steward comes. 1055
Body of me sirs, which way shall I run?   *Run out.*

Enter Covetous.

COVETOUS.

God speed you, what mean you? Would you speak with me?

TENANT.

Yea sir, even to desire your worship my vriend vor to be.

1058. vor to be] *this edn.*; vor to to
be *Q.*

1049. *lightly*] commonly.   1049. *rate*] manner.
1051. *saith Christ*] Luke 12:20.

Ich have a zertain petition to your maship to move,

And ich desire you to be my friend in it vor God's love.　1060

COVETOUS.

What is the matter? Let me know it at once.

I have somewhat else to do than here to tread the stones.

TENANT.

By my truth sir, I beseech you vor me to speak a good word

To your good master and my landlord.

Ich have dwelt in his house this vorty years almost,　　1065

And thereupon chave bestowed much money and cost;

And now ich hear zay ich must double my rent,

Or else void out of it and that incontinent.

I beseech you vor God's sake on me take some pity and boon.

If I be put out for ever cham undone.　　　　　　　1070

O good sir, I know that you may do much.

COVETOUS.

By my truth, I can do nothing herein,

And, so God help me, I esteem no such matters worth a pin.

By'rlady sir, you have had it a fair season,

And that a man should make what he can of his own it is

　　reason.　　　　　　　　　　　　　　　　　　　1075

I warrant you there be enough that that rent will give.

TENANT.

But they shall never thrive on it then I believe.

1070. ever cham] *this edn.*; euer I
cham *Q*.
1071. much.] *this edn.*; much: *Q. A
line may be missing here. Where a colon*
*or a comma is used to end the last line
of a speech, the first line of the next
speech normally completes the rhyme.*

1059. *maship*] abbreviated form of "mastership," which often implied disrespect.

1065–1070.] The Tenant is voicing the common complaint against "rack-renting." Such complaints were essentially moral rather than economic. As Dickens points out, faced with rising prices, "a landlord who failed to raise rents and entry fines would have been a fool or a saint . . . . The controversy over rent . . . concerns the relations of landlords with tenant farmers who were prospering through the exceptional boom in the prices of farm produce and who naturally wanted the best of both worlds —the new high prices they received, together with their old low rents" (p. 152; cf. pp. 151–154).

1069. *boon*] favor.

1074. *By'rlady*] contraction of "by our Lady."

Ich know what he may do with the house and ground;
He may chance to vind rent enough of vive pound.
COVETOUS.
    Well, care not you for that, if you be a wise man;   1080
    You were best to get one better cheap where you can,
    For I know that so much for it have he may,
    Yea, if it stood empty even this present day.
TENANT.
    Well sir, yet methinks there should be a conscience;
    I think God hateth such covetous, sir by your patience.   1085
COVETOUS.
    Thou art a foolish fellow hereof to me to complain,
    For I meddle with no such matters I tell you plain.
HIRELING (*make much curtsey*).
    Good gentleman, God save your life I pray to our Lord!
    May I be so bold to speak with you(gentleman) one word?
COVETOUS.
    Whither the devil wilt thou? into mouth methink!   1090
    For God's arse, how he smells all of drink.
HIRELING.
    Nay, by my truth sir, I drink none other drink today
    But a little fleet milk mingled with whey.
    For, so God help me, if for drink or meat I should die
    I have not one farthing, any therewith to buy.   1095
    And by my truth sir, this is my suit at this time;
    I served your master in making brick and lime
    Half a year together, not missing one day,
    And by my truth all my wages is yet for to pay.
    And if it please you herein to show me some pleasure,   1100
    The same to my power with like I will measure.
COVETOUS.
    Body of me, what a beggarly knave is here.
    Why, can'st thou not forbear thy money one year?

1080. be] *this edn.*; he *Q*.   1091. arse] *this edn.*; ames *Q*.
1091. For] *this edn.*; Fo *Q*.

    1090. *mouth*] *mouth* was used for the surface opening of a pit or cave, and figuratively for the opening to the pit of hell; cf. "hellmouth" as a traditional piece of stage furniture.
    1093. *fleet*] skimmed.

HIRELING.

    No, by my truth sir, for I have no lands,

    Nor nothing to live upon but only my hands.   1105

    I beseech you be good to me.

COVETOUS.

    Why, I meddle not with such things thou dost know.

HIRELING.

    Yes sir, you are Master Steward I trow.

COVETOUS.

    No faith, I am but Master Receiver;

    I take in all, but by gisse I am no payer.   1110

HIRELING.

    Your master hath a great sort of receivers indeed,

    But not one to pay the hireling his true meed.

          [*Enter*] Worldly Man *all brave.*

WORLDLY MAN.

    What, worthy Policy? What make you here today?

COVETOUS.

    About your affairs I have business this way.

    And behold sir, as I traveled the street,   1115

    With these two fellows I chanced for to meet,

    Who told me that they had an earnest suit to you;

    One for his house that he dwelleth in now,

    Wherein (he saith) you go about to do him much wrong,

    For he saith that he hath dwelt in it very long;   1120

    The other said you owe him a piece of money:

    He wrought with you half a year and had never a penny.

    And thus they took on with me before you did come,

    And now have I showed you the whole circumstance and sum.

WORLDLY MAN.

    Marry, hang them, villains! Have I naught to do   1125

    But to stand and reason matters with them two?

1106. me.] *this edn.*; me· *Q. If this is*   *Cf. textual note to l. 1071.*
a broken colon rather than an inverted   1112.1.] All braue Worldly man.
period, a line may have been dropped.   *Q.*

    1104–1105.] The lines reflect the problems in the transitional economy
of the sixteenth century for artisans who owned no land.

    1112. *meed*] wages, reward.

Hear you Tenant, in few words you know my mind;
According as I have told you, so you shall me find.
Other provide money your lease to renew,
Or else you shall out incontinent; this is true.   1130

TENANT.

O landlord, methinks this is too much extremity.
Alas, upon mine age take you some pity.
Cham old and have many children and much charge;
I trust landlord ich shall vind you better at large.

WORLDLY MAN.

I cannot tell what I should do more, believe me;   1135
Many landlords would not do as I do by thee,
For I am content for money thou shouldst have it before
     another.
I can do no more for thee if thou wert my brother.

COVETOUS.

Thou must be answer'd, father, there is no remedy;
By Saint Ann methink he speaketh very reasonably.   1140

TENANT.

This reasonable speaking cometh from an unreasonable
     mind.
Woe be to him that to such inconveniences shall a man bind.

HIRELING.

If it please you sir, help me to my money if you may.

WORLDLY MAN.

No, by my faith sir, you get it not today.
You shall tarry my leisure. I will pay you when I see cause. 1145

HIRELING.

You are happy sir; in your hands you have the laws.
But by gisse, if I had any thing that would do you pleasure,
You should have it when you would and not tarry my
     leisure.
Well, I believe verily that the prayers of the poor and his
     cry
Shall ascend into the ears of the Lord God on high,   1150
And he will plague all those that righteousness withstand,

1130. is] *this edn.*; ts *Q*.

1129–1130. *Other . . . Or*] equivalent to modern English "either . . . or."
1134. *at large*] at length.

And as the prophet saith, root their posterity out of the land.
TENANT.

Well Hireling, let us depart this place;

It prevaileth not us of him to crave any grace.
HIRELING.

No more shall it prevail him, the Scripture saith indeed,   1155

To ask mercy of the Lord when he standeth in need.

Exeunt.

WORLDLY MAN.

Ha, ha, ha. I must laugh, so God me save,

To see what a sort of suitors nowadays we have.
COVETOUS.

I warrant you, if you will be ruled by Reason and Policy,

You shall have all the world to sue to you shortly.   1160
WORLDLY MAN.

A common saying, the fox fareth the better and not the worse

When that the good wife doth him ban and curse.

So what care I, though to curse me the people do not cease,

As long as by them my riches doth increase?

O Policy, how glorious my buildings do shine!   1165

No gentleman's in this country like unto mine.

Sirrah, what shall I do? I must make my barns more great,

For I have not room enough to lay in my rye and wheat.
COVETOUS.

Set men a-work with it as soon as ye can;

If you lack room, make more you may then.   1170
WORLDLY MAN.

By gisse I will, they shall in hand tomorrow.

1152. *prophet saith*] Psalm 37:22 and 28.

1155. *Scripture*] cf. the service "A Commination against Sinners" 1552/
1559 Prayer Books ("The First Day of Lent" in 1549 Prayer Book): "Then
shall it be too late to knock when the door be shut, and too late to cry
mercy when it is the time of justice."

1161. *common saying*] Tilley, F 632.

1165–1168] cf. Latimer, "Sermon XIV" (Parker Society, XXVII, 280):
"All the affections of men now-a-days is in building gay and sumptuous
houses, it is in setting up and pulling down, and never have they done
building. But the end of all such great riches and covetousness is this:
'This night, thou fool, thy soul shall be taken from thee.'" Both Latimer
and Wager are drawing upon the parable of the rich man who destroys
his barns in order to build bigger ones (Luke 12:16–20); cf. l. 1051.

I thank you Policy I need nothing to borrow.
Sirrah, the little tenement that by my house doth stand,
I would I could get that too, even out of hand.
I want a little buttery to lay in my drink,   1175
And that would serve the turn handsomely I think.
And to say the truth, it is not meet that such a beggar as he
Should dwell so near under the nose of me.
COVETOUS.
    Who the devil put that into your mind?
WORLDLY MAN.
    Marry, even that did Reason my trusty friend.   1180
COVETOUS.
    I have been about it myself all this week;
    Ready Wit all the laws for to delay doth seek.
    We will have it, I warrant you, by hook or by crook.
    Tush, I warrant you for such odd ends daily we look.
PROPHET (*without*).
    O thou earth, earth, earth! hear the word of the Lord;   1185
    Know thyself to be no better than clay or dust.

Let the Worldly Man *look suddenly about him.*

    See that thy life to God's truth do always accord:
    For from earth thou camest and to earth thou must.
COVETOUS.
    What is the matter? Why, what ail ye? Why look you so
        about?
WORLDLY MAN.
    I heard a terrible noise, surely without doubt,   1190
    Which pronounced the words of the prophet Jeremy,
    Saying earth, earth, turn thee speedily.
COVETOUS.
    Why, and are you afraid and amazed at that?
    I see well you have a heart like a gnat.

1194. gnat] *this edn.*; Guat *Q*.

1173.] cf. Ahab's design on Naboth's vineyard, I Kings 21 (Craik,
p. 107).
    1175. *buttery*] storage room for liquor or provisions in general.
    1185. *O thou earth*] Jeremiah 22:29.
    1188.] The language here echoes Genesis 3:19.

[*Enter* Prophet.]

PROPHET.

That servant that diligently doth fulfill   1195
And watcheth at all times for the coming of his master,
And doth in the mean season apply his will
Of his master's goods—there be no spoiler nor waster—
That servant shall be sure to be a taster
Of God's blessings and joys everlasting   1200
Whereas is all consolation and nothing wanting.
But that servant that liveth idly without care
And looketh not diligently upon his office,
His master shall come suddenly, or he be aware,
And shall minister to him according to justice.   1205
The portion of hypocrites shall be his;
Into utter darkness cast him out will he
Whereas weeping and gnashing of teeth shall be.   *Exit.*

COVETOUS.

O sirrah, marry, God's blessing on his heart:
Full honestly he teacheth you sir, their part.   1210

WORLDLY MAN.

These be the words of the Holy Scripture
Declaring the difference between the just and unpure.
Good Lord, I would know what these words do mean.

COVETOUS.

Your chaplain can tell you, for he is very well seen.

WORLDLY MAN.

I pray you Policy, call him to me hither,   1215
But look that you come again both together.

COVETOUS.

Yes that we will I warrant, you need not to fear;
We will be here again or a horse can lick his ear.   [*Exit.*]

WORLDLY MAN.

By my truth, methinks I begin to wax sick.
In sending away my counselor I was somewhat too quick. 1220
Well, I will sit me down and say to sleep here

1198. spoiler] *this edn.*; spoile *Q*.

1202–1208.] cf. Luke 12:46 and Math. 25:30.
1214. *well seen*] well-versed.
1221. *say*] try; aphetic form of "assay."

Till they into this place again do appear. O my head.

Enter God's Plague *and stand behind him awhile before he speak.*

GOD'S PLAGUE.

It is even I that upon thee doth blow,
Filling thee with plagues and sundry disease.
What I am, indeed I will learn thee to know,   1225
For I am not afraid thee to displease.
Thou shalt depart from thy house and land,
Thy wife and children beggars thou shalt leave,
Thy life thou shalt lose even out of hand,
And after death thy just reward receive.   1230
Thy ill-gotten goods shall not thee deliver,
Thine costly buildings shall nothing prevail,
Thy odors, thy sweet smells and thou shalt perish together,
Thy rings, thy bracelets, and gold chains shall fall.
Strangers and those whom thou didst never know   1235
Shall possess that which by fraud thou hast got;
Thy seed from off thy ground God will overthrow
Because at his prophet's preaching thou amendest not.
Thou sleepest in death as the prophet David doth say;
Out of which sleep when thou shalt awake   1240
Thou shalt perceive thou must needs away,
And that on thee God will no mercy take.
I am the plague of God properly called
Which cometh on the wicked suddenly;
I go through all towns and cities strongly walled,   1245
Striking to death, and that without all mercy.
Here thou wicked, covetous person I do strike,
Which once on the plow had'st taken hold,
But willingly again thou rannest in the dike;

1238. amendest] *this edn.*; amend-
dest *Q*.

1239. *prophet David*] Psalm 13:3: "Consider, and heare me, O Lorde my God: lyghten myne eyes, that I slepe not in death." The gloss for the last phrase reads: "It is sayd that we slepe in death, when we die, or be slayn of our enemies . . ." (Bible, 1551).
1248.] Luke 9:62.
1249. *dike*] ditch.

Therefore, thy plague shall be doubled sevenfold.   1250

Go out and stand at the door.

[*Enter* Covetous *and* Ignorance.]

COVETOUS.

Come Sir Nicholas, come Sir Nicholas, come Sir Nicholas,
come!

IGNORANCE.

Cham faint by gisse, would ich had a little more bum.

COVETOUS.

A pestilence take thee, hast thou not enough yet?

IGNORANCE.

No, I can drink a gallon and eat never a bit.

COVETOUS.

Come in the knave's name. You must expound a matter.   1255

IGNORANCE.

I can expound good ale from fair water.

COVETOUS.

Tush fellow, thou must expound a piece of scripture.

IGNORANCE.

I can do it as well as any bishop I am sure.

I have spouted with the Genevians, twenty on a row.

COVETOUS.

And thou wert too good for them all, I trow.   1260

IGNORANCE.

Was I? yea, faith that I was, you shall understand
With a piece of Latin I set them all on dry land.

COVETOUS.

And I pray thee heartily, what was it? Let me hear?

1250.1.] *Q prints to the right of ll.*   1262. on] *this edn.*; one *Q.*
1250–1251.

1250.1.] This player (God's Plague) will appear shortly as the Physician
(Craik, p. 33).

1252. *bum*] drink.

1256. *expound*] explain or differentiate, with perhaps an allusion to
interpreting the Miracle at Cana, where Christ changed water into wine.

1259. *spouted*] declaimed; as *OED* points out, in J. Heywood's *Spider and
Flie* (1555), xxxix, 4, "sput" is used by an ignorant speaker in place of
"spute" or "dispute."

1259. *Genevians*] Protestants influenced by Calvin.

1259. *on a row*] in a line.

IGNORANCE.

Thou shalt, if thou wilt promise to give me a pot of beer.
Magistrorum clericium inkepe miorum   1265
Totus perus altus, yongus et oldus
Multus knavoribus et quoque fasorum
Pickpursus omnius argentus shavus et polus.
Let me see what they are all able to say to this.

COVETOUS.

For out of doubt a worthy piece of learning it is.   1270

IGNORANCE.

A man may as much edifying out of my Latin take
As ye may out of expositions that many ministers make.

COVETOUS.

Even as thou say'st, in faith, much of a kind,
For they place the scriptures as feathers in the wind.
Peace, body of me, our master is asleep.   1275

IGNORANCE.

Marry, it was time indeed for us silence to keep.

WORLDLY MAN.

O, I would if I could, but now it is too late.
Hold thy peace I pray thee, and do me no more rate.

COVETOUS.

To whom speak you, sir? to him or to me?

WORLDLY MAN.

There is no remedy now man, and that thou dost see.   1280

IGNORANCE.

Passion of me, sirrah! He dreameth methink.

WORLDLY MAN.

Is there no remedy but to hell I must needs sink?

COVETOUS.

For my life Devotion, he is haunted with the mare.

IGNORANCE.

Nay, it is some worser thing truly I fear.

1279. you, sir?] *this edn.*; you to
Sir? *Q*.

1265–1268.] The lines are untranslatable; at times Latin endings have
been foisted onto English words. The obvious nonsense of the lines points
up the comedy in the situation.
1278. *rate*] berate.
1283. *mare*] goblin, specter; cf. "nightmare."

COVETOUS.

I hold a crown he is not very well. 1285

IGNORANCE.

So methinks, for he dreameth of going to hell.

COVETOUS.

We will wake him out of that troublesome sleep.

IGNORANCE.

Good Lord, seest thou not? Behold how he doth weep.

COVETOUS.

How do you, good master? —Is he asleep or awake?

WORLDLY MAN.

O good Lord, how my heart doth ache. 1290

O, sick, sick, never so sick in my life before.

Good Lord, Policy, I think I shall never go home more.

IGNORANCE.

Marry, God forbid! Why where is your grief?

WORLDLY MAN.

All the parts of my body wanteth relief.

O Devotion, I have such pains in my head 1295

That truly, truly, I wish myself even dead.

COVETOUS.

Methought you dreamed, for to yourself you did talk.

WORLDLY MAN.

Indeed sir, I dreamed I had a great journey to walk.

O what great pains and torments I thought myself in,

Lying in fire which to burn did never lin, 1300

And methought before me the Plague of God did stand

Ready to strike me with a sword in his hand.

And ever I asked him what was the cause,

He answered that I was a transgressor of God's laws.

But Lord how sick I am, and how terrible is my pain. 1305

No place in my body but sickness therein doth reign.

I like not these foolish dreams, Policy my friend.

COVETOUS.

Tush, a straw, upon them never set your mind.

He that to dreams giveth any confidence or trust,

Without doubt very unquietly live he must. 1310

1291. before.] *this edn.*; berfore: *Q.*

1300. *lin*] cease.

WORLDLY MAN.

O sick, sick, sick, O my head, O my back.

COVETOUS.

What would you have sir? Tell us what you lack?

IGNORANCE.

Is it not best that I call hither a physician,

That he may of your sickness declare the disposition?

WORLDLY MAN.

O yea, yea, do so good Devotion, I pray thee Devotion,   1315

God's blessing on thy heart for thy witty motion.

Depart I pray thee with as much haste as may be.

IGNORANCE.

It shall not be long or he be here, you shall see.   *Exit.*

WORLDLY MAN.

O Policy, sick, never so sick. O, hold my head.

O sirrah, what shall become of all my goods when I am

    dead?   1320

COVETOUS.

Dead? body of me, do you reckon to die this year?

Hold your peace, I warrant you, ye need not to fear.

[*Aside.*]   Lo, see you not how the Worldly Man showeth

    his kind?

As sick as he is, on his goods is all his mind.

WORLDLY MAN.

O Policy, if I might not die, what a fellow would I be!   1325

In all this country should be none like unto me.

Sirrah, what a goodly turret have I made in my hall!

But yet my banqueting house pleaseth me best of all.

O, O, alas what a pang is this at my heart.

COVETOUS.

Body of me, aqua-vitae! vinegar! needs help he will depart. 1330

Saint Uncumber be with us, and the blessing of Saint

    Anthony.

1321. reckon] *this edn.*; rocken *Q*.

1327. *turret*] tower or round addition to an angle of a building, frequently
containing a spiral staircase.

1328. *banqueting house*] a separate building, often in the garden, designed
for state receptions and formal dinners. The erection of such a house was
an ostentatious show of wealth.

1330. *aqua-vitae*] unpurified alcohol or liquor.

Help, help our Lady of Walsingham and all her holy
company.

Enter Ignorance [*and* Master Flebishiten, Physician.]

IGNORANCE.

Why, how now? What is the matter? How doth he, Policy?

COVETOUS.

Body of me, help. He is gone else, and that verily.

IGNORANCE.

Stand away foolish knave, and let Master Physician come. 1335

COVETOUS.

Master Flebishiten, should I say, Master Physician, I pray
you look in his bum.

PHYSICIAN.

By your leave my masters, methinks it is no time to jest.
Stand back I pray you, and do not me molest.
Passion of me masters, count you this a play?
One of you quickly bring me hither a key,   1340
Some drink, aqua-vitae if it may be got;
With speed let us have some drink that is hot.

COVETOUS.

Nay, I told you before he was past remedy.

PHYSICIAN.

No, there is life in him yet, I see verily.
Run I pray you, and fetch such things as we lack,   1345
Some drink and a pillow to lay at his back.

IGNORANCE [*run off and back on*].

Here is drink and all things ready at hand.

PHYSICIAN.

Give me room I pray you, out of my light stand.

Be busy and daw him as though he were at dying.

1348.1.] *Q prints to the right of ll.*
1349–1352.

1332. *Lady of Walsingham*] The reference is to the famous shrine of the
Virgin in the north of Norfolk whose image of the Virgin was burnt at
Smithfield during the Reformation.

1340. *key*] Keys have a variety of symbolic meaning in folklore. Although
the significance is not clear here, keys were used in Hebraic tradition to
relieve the agonies of death (cf. G. Jobes, *Dictionary of Mythology, Folklore,
and Symbols* [New York, 1961]).

1348.1. *daw*] revive.

COVETOUS.

Jesu mercy! lo how busy Master Physician is.

Here you sir, is it not best you look on his piss?   1350

PHYSICIAN.

Good fellow be content, I pray thee heartily;

Thou art disposed to jest methink verily.

COVETOUS [aside].

Good fellow? good man hoball! I will make you change your note.

Before that for your labor you get the value of a groat.

PHYSICIAN.

What how, Worldly Man, in God's name I say,   1355

Look up for the love of God, do not like a beast decay.

WORLDLY MAN.

Who is there? What art thou that callest me?

COVETOUS.

Marry Sir, Master Flebishiten, Physician is come, and it was he.

WORLDLY MAN.

O sirs, sirs, I fear me all this labor is in vain;

You might have let me go, I was well out of my pain.   1360

O Master Physician, how think you? what say you to me?

PHYSICIAN.

By my truth, there is no remedy but one that I can see.

You must put your will to God's will, I can say no more.

COVETOUS.

Why, foolish physician, he knew that well enough before.

WORLDLY MAN.

What say'st thou? Is there no remedy but I must die?   1365

PHYSICIAN.

No sir, by my truth, as far as I can see or espy.

God may do much, for he is omnipotent,

But you are past help in this world in man's judgment.

COVETOUS.

What the devil dost thou here? Then get thee away.

WORLDLY MAN.

Depart, physician, and thou hast no more to say.   1370

1353. *hoball*] clown, idiot.

PHYSICIAN.

I trust then, sir, you will content me for my painstaking.

COVETOUS.

You shall have a new loaf at the maid's next baking.

WORLDLY MAN.

Go thy ways, I pray thee and trouble not my mind;
For these news to give thee anything in my heart I cannot
find.

PHYSICIAN.

Good Lord have mercy on thee. Belike it is too late to
amend;   1375
In wickedness thou hast lived, even so thou wilt end.
Gentleman, I trust you will not see me lose my labor.

COVETOUS.

Gentleman, go as you came, you are not so much in my favor.

PHYSICIAN.

A common saying indeed, that is, like unto like,
A wicked master for wicked servants. God must needs
strike.   *Exit.* 1380

WORLDLY MAN.

O sirs, is there no remedy? What shall I say?
Is it not best I set all things at a stay?

COVETOUS.

Yes, make sure work of that whileas you be here.

IGNORANCE.

It is time indeed, for death in you doth appear.

WORLDLY MAN.

Since you know that I am greatly in debt,   1385
And now every one will strive their own for to get,
Bid my wife therefore get a letter of administration as soon
as she may,
And then as she listeth, my creditors she may pay.
Indeed I have enough to pay every man his,
But by Lady, I cannot tell what mine own shall miss.   1390
Commend me to her, and bid her take no thought,

1385. Since] *this edn.*; Once *Q*.

1382. *set . . . stay*] settle matters.
1387. *letter of administration*] authorization to administer the estate of an
intestate in order to avoid the ecclesiastic courts.

But in any wise let her (as near as she can) forgo nought.
COVETOUS.

By my truth, this is wonderfully well invented;
As you have said, I warrant you it shall be frequented.
IGNORANCE.

Your mind in this thing undoubted is not ill;   1395
Now as for other things, it is best you make a will.
WORLDLY MAN.

It shall be, Devotion, even as thou hast said.
Write quickly, for of my life I am afraid.
O must I needs die? O must I needs away?
IGNORANCE.

Here is ink and paper. What shall I write?   1400
WORLDLY MAN.

In the name, first of all do thou indite.
IGNORANCE.

In the name—in, in, in—in the name, what more?
WORLDLY MAN.

Of—   *Fall down.*
IGNORANCE. Of, of, of—what more?
COVETOUS.

Body of me, down with the paper. Away with the ink.
IGNORANCE.

Passion of me, Covetous, he is gone methink.   1405
Hold, hold him. Let us see if any life in him be.
COVETOUS.

Nay hold him that will, the devil hold him for me.
IGNORANCE.

Passion of me, he is dead. How shall we do now?
COVETOUS.

Can'st thou not tell? No more can I, I make God a vow.
Sirrah, here was a trim end that he did make;   1410

1400. and] *this edn.*; aud *Q.*   *part of Worldly Man's preceding*
1403.S.P. IGNORANCE] *Craik; not in*   *speech.*
Q, which prints: Of, of ... more? *as*

1394. *frequented*] commonly practiced.
1401. *In the name*] The common opening formula of a will was "in the name of God. Amen."
1402. *in, in, in*] Ignorance has difficulty spelling and repeats, probably spelling the word out by letters.

Thou never heardst him the name of God in his mouth take.

IGNORANCE.

Tush, God? a straw! His mind was other ways occupied.
All his study was who should have his goods when he died.
Indeed all men may perceive his mind to be corrupt and ill,
For God would not suffer him to name Him in his will.   1415
A strange matter, when men have given over God,
They may be sure to be scourged with His sharp rod.

COVETOUS.

This is the end always where I begin,
For I am the root of all wickedness and sin.
I never rest to teach and instruct men to evil   1420
Till I bring them both body and soul to the devil
As we have done this worldly man here as you see.
Come therefore, Ignorance, wait thou upon me.
The devil and I, thou shalt see, will not leave
Till we have made the greatest part to us to cleave.   1425
Come, let us go hence, here is no more to be said.
Farewell my masters, our parts we have played.   [*Exit ambo.*]

Enter here Satan.

SATAN.

O, O, O, O—all is mine, all is mine.
My kingdom increaseth every hour and day.
O, how they seek my majesty divine;   1430
To come to me they labor all that they may.
The worldly man (quoth he), nay the devilish man then,
For more wickedness and mischief than he did use,
I myself indeed never devise can.
O, at his jolly wisdom I must needs muse.   1435
How cunningly put he his money to usury,
Yea, and that without offence of any law;
He was not to learn any kind of bribery
Whereby wicked gains to him he might draw.
An abominable drunkard, a stinking lecherer,   1440
A filthy sodomite, a corrupt conscience within,
A privy slanderer, and a subtle murderer:

1428. is mine.] *this edn.*; his mine,   1441. conscience] *this edn.*; can-
Q.   science Q.

To be short, a very dunghill and sink of sin.
O my boy Covetous, I may thank thee of all this.
Thou nuzzled'st him in all mischief and vice.   1445
Therefore shalt thou be sure to have my bliss,
For above all other thou indeed art most wise.
Thou teachest the worldly man a leasemonger to be,
To oppress the poor and of his riches him to defraud,
Wickedly to use the laws he learned of thee;   1450
Therefore indeed thou art worthy of much laud.
All you worldly men, that in your riches do trust,
Be merry and jocund, build palaces and make lusty cheer,
Put your money to usury, let it not lie and rust,
Occupy yourselves in my laws while ye be here.   1455
Spare not, nor care not, what mischief you frequent,
Use drunkenness, deceit, take other men's wives,
Pass of nothing—one hour is enough to repent
Of all the wickedness you have done in your lives.
O if you will thus after my laws behave,   1460
You shall have all things as this worldly man had.
Be bold of me, what you will to crave,
And doubt you not but with you I will play the loving lad.
Yea, and after death I will provide a place
For you in my kingdom forever to reign.   1465
You shall fare no worse than doth mine own grace,
That is to lie burning forever in pain.
Come on mine own boy, go thou with me,
Thou hast served me duly and hatest me never;
Therefore now for thy pains rewarded shalt thou be   1470
In everlasting fire that burneth forever.

Bear him out upon his back.

[*Enter* Contentation, Heavenly Man, *and* Enough.]

CONTENTATION.

He that toucheth pitch shall be defiled with the same,
And he that keepeth company with those that be vicious
Shall at the length grow like unto the same,

1446. have] *this edn.*; baue *Q.*

1448. *leasemonger*] one who traffics in leases.
1474. *at the length*] in the end.

Working things wicked and pernicious.   1475
Even so it is also to be associate with the righteous.
For he that haunteth and keepeth honest company
Cannot choose but live according to the same actually.
Example the Jews, being conversant with the heathen,
Drank of their superstition and idolatry,   1480
And by that means fell from the true God of heaven
To worshipping of blocks which was mere blasphemy.
Likewise it is at this day verily,
Christian men are seduced by keeping of ill company,
And brought from the very truth to hypocrisy.   1485
And who are those that are thus deceived?
Even such as are not content when they are well;
They be not thankful for that they have received,
But ever they think still more and more to excel.
Contentation from their minds they do expel,   1490
And under the pretense of reason, wit and policy,
They covet to run to mischief and sin headily.

HEAVENLY MAN.

Like as gold and silver is tried in the fire,
So faithful men in the furnace of adversity be proved.
The heavenly must not live as flesh and lust doth desire,   1495
But heavenly things of heavenly men be loved.
With no kind of temptation he must be moved,
Be it sickness or poverty or whatsoever of God is sent.
The heavenly must take it patiently and be therewith
        content.

ENOUGH.

Enough is as good as a feast where Contentation doth dwell, 1500
For where he remaineth is the spirit of God with rest;
The unquiet mind of the covetous doth grutch and swell,
And to live with Enough he doth abhor and detest.
The greedy grasping of Covetous doth him so molest
That to be rich he all his whole mind doth set,   1505
Nothing regarding how the same he doth get.

CONTENTATION.

Pythagorous saith that a man of covetous desire

1487. they] *this edn.*; to Q.   1504. grasping] *this edn.*; gasping Q.

Cannot be contented neither with abundance,
For the more he hath the more still he doth require,
Wherefore such persons provoke God to vengeance;   1510
Example of the Worldly Man, late of remembrance,
Whose wicked life offended the Lord so exceedingly
That his heavy plagues came upon him suddenly.

HEAVENLY MAN.

God grant his end, example may be
To all men how their riches they shall use.   1515
Make not that thy God which should be servant unto thee,
For in so doing thou dost it greatly abuse.
I pray God (I say) that our covetous we may refuse,
And one of us to love another, for that pleaseth God best;
So shall we be sure to inherit the good land of rest.   1520

[*Enter* Rest.]

REST.

By God's great goodness I am sent unto thee;
Rest is my name wherein the heavenly shall abide.
Happy are those persons that come unto me,
For I being present all troubles I do divide.
With joys I am adorned, yea on every side,   1525
Which are prepared for the heavenly from the beginning,
And given unto them for a reward of their godly living.

HEAVENLY MAN.

Thanks be given to thee O Father omnipotent;
Thy mercies, Lord, and not my deserts truly
Hath caused those joys to me to be sent.   1530
Grant me grace therefore to praise thy name duly;
Thy goodness appeareth to me every day newly.
Whilst breath and life prolong my days,
My mouth shall not cease thy holy name to praise.

ENOUGH.

Enough is as good as a feast. Here let us stay.   1535
We have troubled our audience, that let us remember.
Let us conclude therefore, but first let us pray
That it will please God in mercy our good mistress to tender,

---

1508. *neither*] not used here as correlative, but to strengthen the preceding negative.
1538. *mistress*] Queen Elizabeth.

Our faith to stablish wherein we be slender:
That at the last day when the trump shall blow,   1540
For to be heavenly men the Lord may us all know.

CONTENTATION.

First let us call to God for Jesu Christ's sake
Long to preserve Elizabeth, our most noble Queen.
Good Lord grant her highness the heavenly path to take,
And that all by-ways of her highness may be seen.   1545
Increase her wealth, prolong her health, preserve her life:
That long she may rule this realm without debate or strife.

FINIS

1539. *slender*] deficient.

Appendix

Chronology

Approximate years are indicated by *, occurrences in doubt by (?).

Political and Literary Events	*Works of W. Wager*

1558
Accession of Queen Elizabeth I.
Robert Greene born.
Thomas Kyd born.

1560
George Chapman born.

1561
Francis Bacon born.

1564
Shakespeare born.
Christopher Marlowe born.

1567

*THE LONGER THOU LIVEST THE MORE FOOL THOU ART.**

1570
Thomas Heywood born.*

*ENOUGH IS AS GOOD AS A FEAST.**

1572
Thomas Dekker born.*
John Donne born.
Massacre of St. Bartholomew's Day.

1573
Ben Jonson born.*

1576
The Theatre, the first permanent public theater in London, established by James Burbage.
John Marston born.

1577

The Curtain theater opened.

Holinshed's *Chronicles of England, Scotland and Ireland*.

Drake begins circumnavigation of the earth; completed 1580.

1578

John Lyly's *Euphues: The Anatomy of Wit*.

1579

John Fletcher born.

Sir Thomas North's translation of Plutarch's *Lives*.

1580

Thomas Middleton born.

1583

Philip Massinger born.

1584

Francis Beaumont born.*

1586

Death of Sir Philip Sidney.

John Ford born.

1587

The Rose theater opened by Henslowe.

Marlowe's *TAMBURLAINE*, Part I.*

Execution of Mary, Queen of Scots.

Drake raids Cadiz.

1588

Defeat of the Spanish Armada.

Marlowe's *TAMBURLAINE*, Part II.*

1589

Greene's *FRIAR BACON AND FRIAR BUNGAY*.*

Marlowe's *THE JEW OF MALTA*.*

Kyd's *THE SPANISH TRAGEDY*.*

1590

Spenser's *Faerie Queene* (Books I–III) published.

Sidney's *Arcadia* published.

Shakespeare's *HENRY VI*, Parts I–III,* *TITUS ANDRONICUS.*

1591
Shakespeare's *RICHARD III.*

1592
Marlowe's *DOCTOR FAUSTUS* and *EDWARD II.*
Shakespeare's *TAMING OF THE SHREW* and *THE COMEDY OF ERRORS.*
Death of Greene.

1593
Shakespeare's *LOVE'S LABOR'S LOST;* *Venus and Adonis* published.
Death of Marlowe.
Theaters closed on account of plague.

1594
Shakespeare's *TWO GENTLE-MEN OF VERONA;* *The Rape of Lucrece* published.
Shakespeare's company becomes Lord Chamberlain's Men.
Death of Kyd.

1595
The Swan theater built.
Sidney's *Defense of Poesy* published.
Shakespeare's *ROMEO AND JULIET,* *A MIDSUMMER NIGHT'S DREAM,* *RICHARD II.*
Raleigh's first expedition to Guiana.

1596
Spenser's *Faerie Queene* (Books IV–VI) published.
Shakespeare's *MERCHANT OF VENICE,* *KING JOHN.*
James Shirley born.

1597
Bacon's *Essays* (first edition).
Shakespeare's *HENRY IV*, Part I.*

1598

Demolition of The Theatre.

Shakespeare's *MUCH ADO ABOUT NOTHING,* HENRY IV,* Part II.*

Jonson's *EVERY MAN IN HIS HUMOR* (first version).

Seven books of Chapman's translation of Homer's *Iliad* published.

1599

The Paul's Boys reopen their theater.

The Globe theater opened.

Shakespeare's *AS YOU LIKE IT,* HENRY V, JULIUS CAESAR.**

Marston's *ANTONIO AND MELLIDA,** Parts I and II.

Dekker's *THE SHOEMAKERS' HOLIDAY.**

Death of Spenser.

1600

Shakespeare's *TWELFTH NIGHT.**

The Fortune theater built by Alleyn.

The Children of the Chapel begin to play at the Blackfriars.

1601

Shakespeare's *HAMLET,* MERRY WIVES OF WINDSOR.**

Insurrection and execution of the Earl of Essex.

Jonson's *POETASTER.*

1602

Shakespeare's *TROILUS AND CRESSIDA.**

1603

Death of Queen Elizabeth I; accession of James VI of Scotland as James I.

Florio's translation of Montaigne's *Essays* published.

Shakespeare's *ALL'S WELL THAT ENDS WELL.**
Heywood's *A WOMAN KILLED WITH KINDNESS.*
Marston's *THE MALCONTENT.**
Shakespeare's company becomes the King's Men.

1604
Shakespeare's *MEASURE FOR MEASURE,** *OTHELLO.**
Marston's *THE FAWN.**
Chapman's *BUSSY D'AMBOIS.**

1605
Shakespeare's *KING LEAR.**
Marston's *THE DUTCH COURTESAN.**
Bacon's *Advancement of Learning* published.
The Gunpowder Plot.

1606
Shakespeare's *MACBETH.**
Jonson's *VOLPONE.**
Tourneur's *REVENGER'S TRAGEDY.**
The Red Bull theater built.
Death of John Lyly.

1607
Shakespeare's *ANTONY AND CLEOPATRA.**
Beaumont's *KNIGHT OF THE BURNING PESTLE.**
Settlement of Jamestown, Virginia.

1608
Shakespeare's *CORIOLANUS,** *TIMON OF ATHENS,** *PERICLES.**
Chapman's *CONSPIRACY AND TRAGEDY OF CHARLES, DUKE OF BYRON.**
Dekker's *Gull's Hornbook* published.
Richard Burbage leases Blackfriars theater for King's company.
John Milton born.

1609

Shakespeare's *CYMBELINE*;* *Sonnets* published.
Jonson's *EPICOENE*.

1610

Jonson's *ALCHEMIST*.
Chapman's *REVENGE OF BUSSY D'AMBOIS*.*
Richard Crashaw born.

1611

Authorized (King James) Version of the Bible published.
Shakespeare's *THE WINTER'S TALE*,* *THE TEMPEST*.*
Beaumont and Fletcher's *A KING AND NO KING*.
Middleton's *A CHASTE MAID IN CHEAPSIDE*.*
Tourneur's *ATHEIST'S TRAGEDY*.*
Chapman's translation of *Iliad* completed.

1612

Webster's *THE WHITE DEVIL*.

1613

The Globe theater burned.
Shakespeare's *HENRY VIII* (with Fletcher).
Webster's *THE DUCHESS OF MALFI*.*
Sir Thomas Overbury murdered.

1614

The Globe theater rebuilt.
The Hope theater built.
Jonson's *BARTHOLOMEW FAIR*.

1616

Publication of Folio edition of Jonson's *Works*.
Chapman's *Whole Works of Homer*.
Death of Shakespeare.
Death of Beaumont.

1618
Outbreak of Thirty Years War.
Execution of Raleigh.

1620
Settlement of Plymouth, Massachusetts.

1621
Middleton's *WOMEN BEWARE WOMEN.**
Robert Burton's *Anatomy of Melancholy* published.
Andrew Marvell born.

1622
Middleton and Rowley's *THE CHANGELING.**
Henry Vaughan born.

1623
Publication of Folio edition of Shakespeare's *COMEDIES, HISTORIES, AND TRAGEDIES.*

1625
Death of King James I; accession of Charles I.
Death of Fletcher.

1626
Death of Tourneur.
Death of Bacon.

1627
Death of Middleton.

1628
Ford's *THE LOVER'S MELANCHOLY.*
Petition of Right.
Buckingham assassinated.

1631
Shirley's *THE TRAITOR.*
Death of Donne.
John Dryden born.

1632
Massinger's *THE CITY MADAM.**

1633

Donne's *Poems* published.

Death of George Herbert.

1634

Death of Chapman, Marston, Webster.*

Publication of *THE TWO NOBLE KINSMEN*, with title-page attribution to Shakespeare and Fletcher.

Milton's *Comus*.

1635

Sir Thomas Browne's *Religio Medici*.

1637

Death of Jonson.

1639

First Bishops' War.

Death of Carew.*

1640

Short Parliament.

Long Parliament impeaches Laud.

Death of Massinger, Burton.

1641

Irish rebel.

Death of Heywood.

1642

Charles I leaves London; Civil War breaks out.

Shirley's *COURT SECRET*.

All theaters closed by Act of Parliament.

1643

Parliament swears to the Solemn League and Covenant.

1645

Ordinance for New Model Army enacted.

1646

End of First Civil War.

1647

Army occupies London.

Charles I forms alliance with Scots.

Publication of Folio edition of Beaumont and Fletcher's *COMEDIES AND TRAGEDIES.*

1648
Second Civil War.

1649
Execution of Charles I.

1650
Jeremy Collier born.

1651
Hobbes' *Leviathan* published.

1652
First Dutch War began (ended 1654).
Thomas Otway born.

1653
Nathaniel Lee born.*

1656
D'Avenant's *THE SIEGE OF RHODES* performed at Rutland House.

1657
John Dennis born.

1658
Death of Oliver Cromwell.
D'Avenant's *THE CRUELTY OF THE SPANIARDS IN PERU* performed at the Cockpit.

1660
Restoration of Charles II.
Theatrical patents granted to Thomas Killigrew and Sir William D'Avenant, authorizing them to form, respectively, the King's and the Duke of York's Companies.

1661
Cowley's *THE CUTTER OF COLEMAN STREET.*
D'Avenant's *THE SIEGE OF RHODES* (expanded to two parts).

1662

Charter granted to the Royal Society.

1663

Dryden's *THE WILD GALLANT*. Tuke's *THE ADVENTURES OF FIVE HOURS*.

1664

Sir John Vanbrugh born.

Dryden's *THE RIVAL LADIES*. Dryden and Howard's *THE INDIAN QUEEN*.

Etherege's *THE COMICAL RE-VENGE*.

1665

Second Dutch War began (ended 1667).

Great Plague.

Dryden's *THE INDIAN EM-PEROR*.

Orrery's *MUSTAPHA*.

1666

Fire of London.

Death of James Shirley.